AF801084

DISCOVER YOUR & POTENTIAL & FUTURE

A Guide to Life Skills, Personal Growth, and Creating a Future You Love

AGES 11–13

- Discover Your Strengths
- Make Positive Choices
- Set Goals & Take Action
- Be Kind, Confident & Stay Curious

“Your potential is limitless. Believe in yourself.”

Created by:

Mona Liza Santos

“Your future is yours to create. Make it amazing.”

Copyright © 2026 by Mona Liza Santos

All rights reserved.

No part of this publication may be reproduced, distributed, stored in a retrieval system, or transmitted in any form or by any means, including electronic, mechanical, photocopying, recording, or otherwise, without prior written permission from the publisher, except in the case of brief quotations used in reviews or educational references permitted by copyright law.

Discover Your Potential & Future

A Guide to Life Skills, Personal Growth, and Creating a Future You Love

Written by
Mona Liza Santos

Published by
World Love Press
San Diego, California
United States of America

ISBN: 978-1-959805-75-5

This workbook was created to help young people build confidence, develop important life skills, and make smart choices for a successful and fulfilling future.

The activities and lessons in this workbook are designed to support personal growth, financial smarts, goal setting, creativity, and a positive mindset for students, families, schools, workshops, and community programs.

This book is intended for educational and informational purposes only. The lessons, activities, examples, worksheets, and exercises included in this publication are designed to encourage learning, personal development, and critical thinking for young readers.

The characters and scenarios portrayed throughout this book are fictional and created for educational storytelling purposes. Any resemblance to actual persons, living or dead, businesses, organizations, or events is purely coincidental.

The author and publisher do not guarantee specific results or outcomes from the use of this book. Readers are encouraged to seek guidance from trusted adults, educators, or professionals when making important decisions.

Illustrations were created using AI-assisted tools and refined by a human illustrator.

SET GOALS
Plan today for a better tomorrow.

SAVE WISELY
Make smart choices with your money.

GROW YOUR FUTURE
Invest in knowledge, skills, and character.

THINK CREATIVELY
Ideas today can create solutions tomorrow.

LEAD & INSPIRE
Be a leader and make a positive impact.

Printed in the United States of America

DISCOVER YOUR & POTENTIAL & FUTURE

A Guide to Life Skills, Personal Growth, and Creating a Future You Love

AGES 11-13

Middle school is full of bigger choices. As Maya and Mateo grow older, they begin facing real-world money decisions and future-building opportunities.

This workbook was created to help students build practical financial confidence while learning how real-world money choices shape future opportunities.

- Budgeting
- Smart spending
- Banking
- Entrepreneurship
- Credit awareness
- Leadership
- Creativity
- Public speaking
- Wealth-building habits
- Storytelling and self-publishing

Created by:
Mona Liza Santos

Dedication Page

Dream.
Plan.
Act.
Repeat.

Your future is worth the work.

Dedicated to every young dreamer learning that smart choices today can help build a stronger tomorrow.

Small Steps
- ☑ Big Goals
- ☑ Bright Future
- ☑ Keep Going

May you discover the confidence, knowledge, and courage to dream big, spend smart, and build boldly.

Learn
Grow
Succeed

You've got ideas.
You've got potential.
You've got this.

The best investment you can make is in yourself.

Created by
Mona Liza Santos

DREAM BIG.
SPEND SMART.
BUILD BOLDLY.

This Workbook Belongs To:

STUDENT NAME: ______________________________

AGE: ______________________________

GRADE: ______________________________

SCHOOL OR ORGANIZATION: ______________________________

MY BIGGEST DREAM: ______________________________

____

____

____

DREAM BIG REMINDER:

Small smart choices today can help build big dreams tomorrow.

GOALS I WANT TO LEARN:

Circle what excites you most:

- ○ Saving Money
- ○ Budgeting
- ○ Leadership
- ○ Entrepreneurship
- ○ Creativity
- ○ Teamwork
- ○ Goal Setting
- ○ Smart Spending

BONUS ACTIVITY:

Draw yourself as a future leader, entrepreneur, or dream builder!

This workbook is your personal journey toward building confidence, creativity, leadership, and financial success.

How to Use This Workbook

This workbook combines engaging storytelling with real-world financial education.

STORY PAGES

Fallow Maya and Mateo as they face realistic financial situations and middle school challenges.

ADVICE PAGES

Learn practical wisdom from Lola's Wisdom, Lola's Legacy Lessons, Maya's Mistakes, and Mateo's Money Moves.

WORKSHEETS AND MONEY MATH

Practice through budget planners, spending trackers, business builders, reflection activities, discounts, profit, banking, and interest.

FUTURE CEO CHALLENGES

Build mock businesses, public speaking skills, product ideas, business pitches, and leadership confidence.

FINAL GOAL

This workbook helps students become financially smart, entrepreneurial, responsible, creative, and confident leaders.

Maya teaches smart spending, confidence, emotional growth, and leadership.

Mateo teaches discipline, financial strategy, long-term thinking, and creativity.

Together these characters combine family values, financial literacy, entrepreneurship, leadership, and creativity.

Different strengths.
One mission.
A brighter future!

Big Goals.
Smart Choices.
Bright Future!

Meet the Characters

MAYA

Maya is creative, social, and ambitious. She enjoys fun experiences, trends, and creative opportunities. As she grows older, Maya learns that confidence is stronger than pressure.

MATEO

Mateo is thoughtful, strategic, and future-focused. He enjoys saving, budgeting, entrepreneurship, and wealth-building.

LOLA

Lola teaches confidence, patience, emotional discipline, responsibility, and needs vs wants.

LOLO

Lolo teaches budgeting, banking, credit, business, investing, and financial independence.

Maya teaches smart spending, confidence, emotional growth, and leadership.

Mateo teaches discipline, financial strategy, long-term thinking, and creativity.

Together these characters combine family values, financial literacy, entrepreneurship, leadership, and creativity.

Different strengths.
One mission.
A brighter future!

You have dreams.
You have power.
You can build an amazing future!

WELCOME FUTURE LEADERS!

Smart today,
Stronger tomorrow,
Successful always!

Hi there! We're Lola and Lolo, and this is Maya and Mateo!

We created this book just for **YOU**—a future leader with big dreams and endless potential.

Money is a tool. When you learn how to use it wisely, it can help you create freedom, support your dreams, and make a positive difference in the world.

Your future is in your hands!

In this book, you will learn, grow, and discover how to make smart choices with money—so you can build the life you imagine!

Together, we promise to help you:

- Think smarter about money.
- Set goals and chase your dreams.
- Grow your skills and confidence every day.
- Save today for a better tomorrow.
- Make good choices when you spend.
- Use your blessings to help others and lead.

You are capable. You are important. You are the future.

We believe in you, and we're so excited to be part of your journey!

Let's learn. Let's grow. Let's build your amazing future—together!

TABLE OF CONTENTS

CHAPTER / SECTION	PAGE
Chapter 1: Bigger Choices, Bigger Dreams	1
Chapter 2: The Budget Blueprint	13
Chapter 3: Smart Shopping	31
Chapter 4: Earning Money	39
Chapter 5: Mini Business Builder	51
Chapter 6: Banking and Saving	65
Chapter 7: Credit and Borrowing	77
Chapter 8: Bills and Real-Life Expenses	90
Chapter 9: Investing and Growing Money	102
Chapter 10: Storytelling, Branding, and Self-Publishing	113
Certificate of Completion	131
Dear Future Leaders	132
Future Leaders Pledge	133
About the Author	134
My Big Dreams Notes	135
Future Savings Tracker	136
One-Year Goal Tracker	137
My Future Business Ideas	138
Notes Page	139
Notes Page	140

WHAT YOU'LL LEARN IN THIS BOOK

This workbook-storybook will help you build smart money habits, explore entrepreneurship, and develop leadership skills so you can create your own opportunities and a successful future!

YOU WILL LEARN HOW TO:

1. **BUILD SMART MONEY HABITS**
   Understand money basics, create budgets, and learn how to spend, save, and give wisely.

2. **UNDERSTAND BANKING**
   Learn how banks work, different accounts, and how to manage your money safely.

3. **BUILD CREDIT AWARENESS**
   Discover what credit is, why it matters, and how to build good credit for your future.

4. **GROW AN ENTREPRENEUR MINDSET**
   Learn the traits of successful entrepreneurs and how to think creatively and solve problems.

5. **DEVELOP LEADERSHIP & COMMUNICATION SKILLS**
   Build confidence, speak up, work with others, and lead with respect and empathy.

6. **SPARK CREATIVITY & INNOVATION**
   Explore your ideas, think outside the box, and bring creative solutions to life.

7. **START & MANAGE A BUSINESS**
   Learn the steps to start a business, make a plan, set goals, and keep your business growing.

8. **MAKE SMART DECISIONS & TAKE ACTION**
   Learn how to weigh choices, manage risks, and take action toward your goals.

9. **TELL YOUR STORY & SHARE YOUR VOICE**
   Build storytelling skills, express your ideas, and inspire others through your story.

10. **PREPARE FOR YOUR FUTURE**
    Gain the tools and confidence to create your path, make an impact, and build the life you imagine.

Small choices today can shape your future!

Chapter 1

Bigger Choices, Bigger Dreams

Middle school brings bigger decisions, bigger pressures, and bigger opportunities.

As Maya and Mateo enter middle school, life begins to feel very different. Students are paying more attention to shoes, clothes, phones, trends, social status, and popularity.

- Peer pressure
- Social comparison
- Emotional spending
- Confidence challenges
- Bigger financial decisions

Chapter Goal

This chapter helps students understand how outside pressure can influence spending and how true financial confidence begins with thoughtful decision-making.

Think Smart. Choose Wisely. Build Your Future.

Good money habits today create more opportunities tomorrow!

Story

Maya and Mateo were growing up. Middle school felt exciting with new teachers, new friends, and new opportunities. But it also felt overwhelming. The choices seemed bigger. The pressure felt stronger. Suddenly, everyone seemed focused on what they owned.

Some students showed off expensive sneakers. Others compared phones, bags, and brands. Maya noticed how quickly popularity sometimes seemed connected to possessions. For the first time, Maya began to feel pressure. Mateo noticed too, but instead of comparing, he observed quietly.

Lesson Embedded

Middle school often introduces social pressure that can influence financial habits.

Key Takeaway

Not all spending decisions are based on need. Some are based on pressure.

Smart money choices today build a stronger tomorrow! $

Story

At lunch, Maya sat with classmates as conversations quickly turned toward expensive sneakers, new phones, designer backpacks, and popular brands.

"I think I need new shoes," Maya whispered. Mateo looked up from his lunch. "Do you really need them," he asked calmly, "or do you just feel pressured?" Maya paused. Maybe it was comparison. Maybe it was fear of being left out.

Lesson Embedded

Peer pressure can quietly affect spending decisions.

Key Takeaway

Pressure can disguise itself as necessity.

Be kind to your future self. Plan, save, and make choices you'll be proud of!

Story

That question stayed with Maya all day. As she walked through the halls, she began noticing purchases differently. Were they about need, confidence, fitting in, or emotional reactions?

Money choices were not always about money. Sometimes they were about confidence, pressure, emotions, and identity. True confidence could not be purchased.

Main Lesson

Financial literacy also includes emotional awareness.

Key Takeaway

Confidence should not be built through spending.

Lolo's Legacy Lesson: Think Before You Spend

That evening, Lolo sat with Maya and Mateo. "Before you spend," he explained, "pause and ask yourself important questions."

- Do I truly need this?
- Will this help my future?
- Am I buying because of pressure?
- Is this worth my hard work?
- Will I regret this later?

Lolo's Real-World Wisdom

Money should serve your goals, not your insecurities.

Key Lesson

Smart spending is about purpose, not pressure.

Leadership Reminder

Strong leaders make intentional choices even when others follow trends.

Quick Tip!

Wait 24 hours before making a non-essential purchase. You'll make clearer, smarter choices!

Remember:

- Pause before you purchase.
- Understand your real reasons.
- Give yourself time to think.
- Choose what supports your goals and values.

Wise choices today build the life you dream of tomorrow.

Vocabulary Builder

Need	Something necessary for health, safety, learning, or daily life.
Want	Something enjoyable but not essential.
Peer Pressure	Influence from others that affects your choices.
Goal	A future achievement you are working toward.
Decision	A thoughtful choice based on priorities and consequences.
Bonus Tip	Understanding vocabulary strengthens financial confidence.

Remember!

- Pause before you purchase.
- Understand your real reasons.
- Give yourself time to think.
- Stay true to your goals and values.
- Small choices today, big wins tomorrow!

Needs, Wants, or Social Pressure?

Instructions

Read each item carefully. Write N = Need, W = Want, or SP = Social Pressure.

1. Designer sneakers ....
2. Winter coat ....
3. Water bottle ....
4. Popular phone case ....
5. School binder ....
6. Trendy hoodie ....
7. Gaming console ....
8. Healthy lunch ....

Quick Guide

Need (N):
You need it to live, be safe, or learn.

Want (W):
It would be nice to have, but you can live without it.

Social Pressure (SP):
You want it because others might judge you or because it's "trendy."

Reflection Questions

- Which choices support your future?
- Which are influenced by outside pressure?
- How can you strengthen your spending habits?

Lolo's Tip!

Pause, think, and choose what aligns with your goals and values—not what others expect.

Smart choices today. Stronger future tomorrow.

Knowing your triggers helps you make better choices!

My Spending Triggers

Instructions

Circle what most influences your spending.

Friends

Social media

Sales

Emotions

Trends

Boredom

Fear of missing out

You can't always control the trigger, but you can control your choice!

Reflection Questions

- What most affects my choices?
- Have I ever spent money because of pressure?
- How can I improve my confidence?
- What habits would protect my goals?

Lolo's Advice

Pause.
Plan.
Choose what moves you forward.

Try This!

The next time you feel the urge to spend, STOP. Take a deep breath and ask:

"Is this a need, a want, or someone else's influence?"

Understand your triggers. Take back your power. Build your future.

Money Math Practice

Instructions

Maya wants sneakers that cost $80.
She saves $10 each week.

Reflection Questions

- How many weeks will it take Maya to save $80?
- If Maya spends $20 on impulse purchases first, how many extra weeks will she need?
- If Maya saves $15 weekly instead, how much faster can she reach her goal?

Maya's Savings Plan

Goal: Sneakers = $80

Saves: $10 each week

Plan: Save a little each week and stay focused!

Track Maya's Progress!

Week	Amount Saved	Total Saved	Still Need
1	$10	$10	$70
2	$10	$20	$60
3	$10	$30	$50
4	$10	$40	$40
5	$10	$50	$30
6	$10	$60	$20
7	$10	$70	$10
8	$10	$80	$0

☆ Goal Reached!

Did You Know?

The more consistent you are with saving, the easier it gets to reach your goals. Small, steady steps create BIG results!

Money Quote

"The things you want today, can be yours tomorrow."

☆ Smart Saving Tips from Lolo!

Pay yourself first. Save before you spend.

Wait 24 hours. It helps you decide if you really want it.

Make a plan. A plan turns your goals into action.

Celebrate progress! Every step forward is a win!

Plan. Save. Stay focused. Your goals are possible!

Great leaders choose their future over pressure!

What Would You Do?

Instructions

Your friends are all buying expensive new headphones. You are saving for a laptop, a future business, or educational goals.

What Would You Do?

Circle your choice and explain why.

Stay Focused

Keep saving for your goal because it's more important to your future.

OR

Spend Now

Buy the headphones so you don't feel left out.

My choice: ____________ Why? ________________________

____

____

Reflection Questions

- Would you spend or stay focused?
- Why?
- How does confidence protect your future?
- How can planning strengthen your choices?

Bonus Challenge

Sometimes leadership means making wise choices even when they are unpopular.

Think of a time when you made a choice that was hard but the right thing to do.

What happened? How did it help you?

____

____

____

Compare the Results

Small choices today = Big results tomorrow!

If You Stay Focused...

- ✓ You reach your goal faster.
- ✓ You build confidence.
- ✓ You set a powerful example.
- ✓ Your future opens up!

If You Spend Now...

- ✗ It takes longer to reach your goal.
- ✗ You might have regret.
- ✗ It sends the wrong message about your priorities.
- ✗ Opportunities could be missed.

Tips to Stay Strong When You're Tempted

Know Your Why
Remember the big reason you're saving.

Choose Your Circle
Surround yourself with people who support your goals.

Make a Plan
A plan today keeps you on track tomorrow.

Celebrate Small Wins
Every step forward deserves recognition!

Practice Discipline
Discipline today leads to freedom and success tomorrow!

You have the power to choose your future. Stay focused. Keep growing. **Lead the way!**

Smart choices today build the life you want tomorrow!

Money Mission: Pause Before You Purchase

Instructions

Before buying anything this week, ask:

Need? Want? Pressure? Future value?

Is it worth my effort?

Reflection Questions

- Record one purchase decision this week and reflect on whether it aligned with your future goals.
- How did pausing before purchasing make you feel?
- Did you discover anything about your priorities?
- How did your choice impact your budget or savings?

Example Scenario

Maya sees a trendy hoodie for $45.

N Need? → No, she has warm hoodies.

W Want? → Yes, it's cool!

P Pressure? → Her friends have it.

F Future Value? → It won't help her save for her laptop.

E Effort? → She decides to wait.

Maya walks away and puts the $45 toward her laptop goal instead!

The 5 Question Pause

N Need?
Do I really need this?

W Want?
Do I want this, or just like it?

P Pressure?
Am I feeling pressure from others, ads, or emotions?

F Future Value?
Will this help me or my future goals?

E Effort?
Is it worth my time, money, and energy?

If you can't answer YES to your future, maybe wait or walk away.

My Purchase Decision Tracker

Item	Need, Want, or Both?	Did I Feel Pressure?	Will It Help My Future Goals?	Did I Buy It? (Yes/No)	Why or Why Not?

Smart Money Habits to Use Every Day

Check Before You Buy
Compare prices and look for better deals.

Save for Your Goals
Put money aside for things that really matter.

Wait 24 Hours
Give yourself time to decide if it's worth it.

Use Your 5 Questions
Pause and think before you spend.

Celebrate Smart Wins
Every smart choice brings you closer to your dreams!

Track Your Progress
Keep track of your savings and watch your goals grow.

You have the power to choose your future.
Pause. Plan. Purpose. Prosper!

Every step you take today builds the future you imagine!

Chapter 1 Recap

Bigger Choices Require Bigger Thinking

Final Chapter Message

Every wise decision strengthens your financial future.

CONFIDENCE OVER COMPARISON

Confidence comes from within, not from what you own.

Key Lesson:
Be you. It's enough.

PRESSURE IS REAL

Peer pressure and social comparison can lead to poor spending.

Key Lesson:
Pause and think before you spend.

EMOTIONAL AWARENESS

Understanding your emotions helps you make better money decisions.

Key Lesson:
Name your feelings. Choose your actions.

SMART SPENDING PROTECTS GOALS

Smart spending helps you reach your goals faster and with less stress.

Key Lesson:
Spend with a plan, not on impulse.

PURPOSE MATTERS MOST

When your money has a purpose, your choices become more powerful.

Key Lesson:
Choose what aligns with your purpose.

Big Ideas to Remember

- You don't need to fit in to be confident.
- Pause before you purchase.
- Emotions influence your spending.
- Plans protect your future.
- Purpose is more powerful than popularity.

What Did You Learn?

- What was the most important lesson in this chapter?
- How has your thinking about money changed?
- What will you do differently next time you feel pressured?

Your Next Step

Pick one action you will take this week to make a smarter financial choice.

My Action Plan:

Cool Fact!

People who set goals and plan their spending are 2x more likely to reach their goals and feel less stressed about money!

Every wise decision strengthens your financial future.

A plan today means peace of mind tomorrow!

The Budget Blueprint

A budget creates freedom through planning.

Maya begins learning that confidence is not only about what you avoid spending. It is also about knowing how to manage what you earn.

What is a Budget?

A budget is a plan for your money. It helps you decide how to use your money on the things that matter most.

The 4 Money Powers

- **Saving** – Keep money for the future.
- **Spending** – Use money for needs and wants wisely.
- **Giving** – Help others and support causes you care about.
- **Growing** – Make your money work for you.

Helpful Advice #1: Track Your Money

Write down what you earn and spend. Tracking helps you see where your money goes and where you can make better choices.

Helpful Advice #2: Set Priorities

Decide what matters most—needs, goals, and responsibilities—before spending on wants. Your priorities guide your budget.

Helpful Advice #3: Plan Ahead

Plan for regular expenses and unexpected costs. Having a plan helps you avoid stress and stay in control.

Helpful Advice #4: Build Good Habits

Small, consistent habits like saving a little each week or waiting before buying can lead to big success over time.

Try This!

Write down 3 things you spend money on this week. Then, decide which part of the 4 Money Powers they belong to.

Lola's Advice

A budget isn't about limits. It's about choices that move you closer to your dreams.

Family Tip

Talk with your family about your budget. They can inspire you, support you, and help you stay on track!

Small steps today. Big choices tomorrow. Stronger you. Bright future.

Plan today.
Budget wisely.
Build your
brighter future!

Story

Maya admitted her money seemed to disappear quickly. Lolo smiled and placed a notebook on the kitchen table. "Every future needs a plan," he said.

Maya looked confused. "A plan for money?"
Lolo nodded. "Especially for money."

They opened the notebook together. The first page said:

A PLAN TODAY, FREEDOM TOMORROW.

Maya took a deep breath. "I want more freedom—like buying what I love, helping others, and saving for big dreams. But I don't know where to start."

Lolo pulled out a calculator. "Let's build your budget blueprint." Together, they added up her income. Then they planned where it would go.

Saving. Spending. Giving. Growing.

Maya smiled. "This actually makes sense."
Lolo winked. "Because a plan today—
builds a brighter tomorrow."

Lesson Embedded

Financial freedom requires planning.

Key Takeaway

A plan gives you control over your money and your future.

Did You Know?

- Students who budget are more likely to reach their financial goals.
- Even small amounts saved regularly can grow over time.
- Planning now helps you handle surprises later.

Money Management Tips

- **Track your money** – Know where it comes from and where it goes.
- **Use needs vs. wants** – Focus on needs first, wants later.
- **Set goals** – Short-term and long-term goals keep you motivated.
- **Save first** – Pay yourself before you spend.
- **Prepare for the unexpected** – Keep an emergency fund.

Build It into a Habit

Make budgeting a part of your routine!

- Review your plan weekly.
- Adjust as your needs change.
- Celebrate small wins.
- Stay consistent and keep learning!

Reflection Time

- What surprised you about Maya's story?
- How can a plan help you feel more in control?
- What is one goal you want to save for?
- How will you start your own budget plan?

Small steps today can lead to big wins tomorrow!

Story

"A budget tells your money where to go," Lolo explained.
He divided the notebook into four categories: saving, spending, giving, and growing.
Maya realized budgeting was not about restriction.
It was about creating control.

The 4 Budget Categories

Saving – Set aside money for goals, emergencies, and the future.

Spending – Use money for things you need and enjoy, but make smart choices.

Giving – Support causes and people that matter to you.

Growing – Invest in yourself by learning new skills and building wealth.

Why Budgeting Matters

- It helps you reach your goals.
- It prepares you for real-life responsibilities.
- It builds confidence in your decisions.
- It helps you handle unexpected situations.
- It teaches you to make your money work for you.

Income vs. Expenses

Your income is the money you receive.

Your expenses are the money you spend.

Goal:

Spend less than you earn so you can save and grow.

Needs vs. Wants

Needs	Wants
Things you must have to live and function.	Things you would like to have but can live without.
• Food • Shelter • Clothing • Transportation • School supplies	• New gadgets • Designer clothes • Entertainment • Eating out • Trendy items

Tip: Focus on needs first, then budget for wants.

Budgeting in Real Life

Budgeting isn't just for big adults. You already use money every day! Whether it's allowance, gifts, or money from a job, a budget helps you:

- Make better choices
- Avoid running out of money
- Feel less stressed
- Be ready for opportunities

Smart Money Habits

1. Think before you spend.
2. Stick to your plan.
3. Save a little, even if it's small.
4. Learn from mistakes.
5. Keep your goal in mind.

Good habits today build a better future!

Challenge Time!

Your Challenge: Create a simple budget for one week using the four categories.

Try It:

1. Write down your income.
2. Decide how much to put in each category.
3. Track your spending.
4. See what you can improve!

Make a plan. Take action. Stay consistent. Create your future.

Little choices today shape your tomorrow!

Story

That evening, Maya added up her small purchases. Snacks, accessories, impulse buys, and extra treats had quietly used up her money. "I spent all that?" she asked.

Lolo nodded gently. "Small habits can either build your future or quietly delay it."

Where Does Money Disappear?

Small amounts may not seem like much, but they can add up fast!

- Snacks and drinks
- Accessories
- Impulse buys
- Extra treats

Helpful Reminders

- Track your spending so nothing sneaks by.
- Pause before you buy. Do you really need it?
- Trade "want now" for "goal later."
- Small savings today = big success tomorrow.

Think Before You Spend

Ask yourself these 3 questions:

1. Do I need this?
2. Can I afford this?
3. Will this help or hurt my goals?

Good Habits Build Your Future

Every time you make a smart choice with money, you are:

- ✓ Staying in control
- ✓ Getting closer to your goals
- ✓ Building the future you want

Try It Yourself!

Look back at your recent spending. Write down 3 small things you spent money on this week. Could you have saved or made a different choice for any of them?

1. ____________________
2. ____________________
3. ____________________

Did You Know?

Cutting just $1 a day in extra spending can save you more than $365 a year!

Reflection Time

Take a moment to think...

- What did you learn about your spending?
- What small change can you make starting today?
- How will that help you in the future?

Smart choices now. Better days ahead. Your future, your way.

Every smart choice today creates more freedom tomorrow!

Lola's Wisdom: A Budget Builds Freedom

"Budgeting is not about saying no to everything," Lola explained. "It is about making sure your money supports what matters most."

- Awareness
- Control
- Confidence
- Opportunity

Real-World Wisdom

When you budget, you tell your money where to go instead of wondering where it went.

Key Lesson

A budget is not restriction.
It is freedom with direction.

Lola's Top Tips

- Know what matters most to you.
- Plan your money on purpose.
- Stay in control of your choices.
- Build confidence with each decision.
- Look for opportunities to grow.

Budgeting Gives You Freedom To:

- Reach your goals
- Make choices you feel good about
- Handle surprises
- Help others
- Invest in your future

Remember:

A good budget helps your money work for you, not the other way around.

Cool Facts!

- People who budget are less stressed and more confident about their future.
- Even small amounts saved regularly can grow into big opportunities (overtime).
- Tracking your money helps you spot patterns and make better choices.
- A budget is a plan that protects your dreams and prepares you for the unexpected!

Try It!

Write down one thing you care about most.
How can budgeting help you make it happen?

1. ____________
2. ____________
3. ____________

Did You Know?

A $5 saving a day is $35 a week and about $1,820 a year!
Small steps lead to big results.

Reflection Questions

- What are the 4 benefits Lola shared?
- How does budgeting give you freedom?
- What is one opportunity you want to create with your money?

My Notes ____

Dream bigger. Budget better. Make it happen.

VOCABULARY BUILDER

	Budget	A plan for how money is earned, saved, spent, and grown.
	Income	Money earned or received.
	Expense	Money spent.
	Savings	Money set aside for future goals.
	Giving	Money used to help others or meaningful causes.
	Growing	Money used to build future wealth through smart financial choices.

BONUS TIP

Understanding vocabulary strengthens financial confidence.

MORE FINANCIAL TERMS TO KNOW

	Need	Something you must have to live, stay healthy, and take care of responsibilities.
	Want	Something you would like to have but can live without.
	Goal	A plan for something you want to achieve in the future.
	Prioritize	To decide what is most important and focus on that first.
	Save	To set money aside instead of spending it now.
	Invest	To use money to earn more over time through smart choices.
	Debt	Money you borrow that you need to pay back.
	Future Value	The amount your money can grow to be worth over time.

SMART MONEY HABITS

- Track your money so you know where it goes.
- Spend on needs first, then wants.
- Save a little regularly, even if it's not much.
- Use your money to reach your goals.
- Think before you spend.

WHY IT MATTERS

- Good money habits create less stress.
- You can handle surprises.
- You get closer to your dreams.
- You have more choices in the future.
- You build confidence in your decisions.

Learn it. Use it. Grow with it. Create your future.

My Weekly Budget Tracker

Instructions

Imagine you earn or receive money each week.
Create your budget plan.

Weekly Income	$ ________
Saving	$ ________
Spending	$ ________
Giving	$ ________
Growing	$ ________

Tip of the Week

A good budget isn't about having more money.
It's about making the most of what you have!

Reflection Questions

- Did my budget reflect my priorities?
- Did I save enough?
- What category needs improvement?
- What can I do differently next week?

Think About It!

When you save consistently, it adds up.

Smart Budgeting Tips

- Track your income and expenses.
- Set goals for your money.
- Save a little each week.
- Avoid impulse spending.
- Give to others when you can.
- Invest in your future.

Where Does My Money Go?

Fill in the % of your plan.

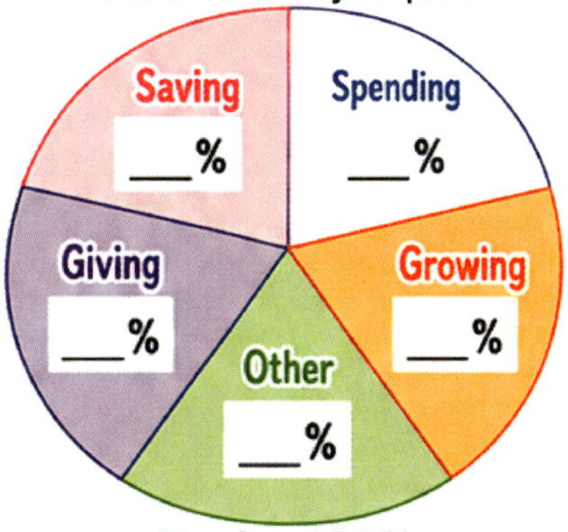

Total = 100%

Are you ready to stick to a plan on saving?

- ○ Yes! I'm ready to do this!
- ○ I think so, I'll try my best.
- ○ Not sure yet, I need a plan.
- ○ Not right now.

What will help you stay on track?

____

____

____

Budget Pie Chart Challenge

Instructions

You have $50. Divide your money into saving, spending, giving, and growing.
Decide how much you want to put in each category.
Then, fill in the amounts and create your pie chart below.

Saving $ ________

Spending $ ________

Giving $ ________

Growing $ ________

Reminder:
$50.00 is 100% of your money.
Make sure your amounts add up to $50.00!

Create Your Pie Chart

Use the space below to show how you divided your $50.

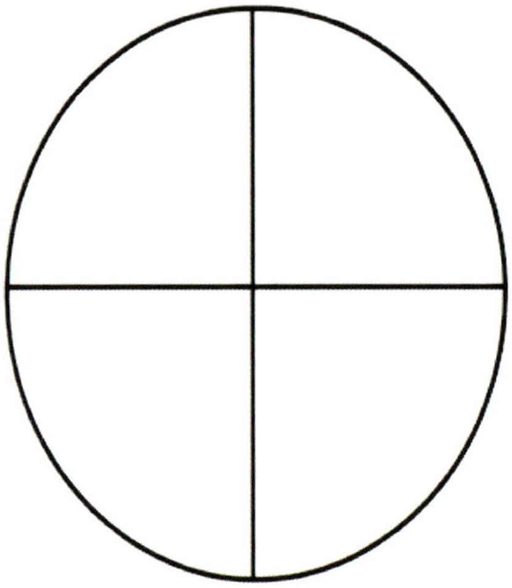

Saving ______ %

Spending ______ %

Giving ______ %

Growing ______ %

Total 100%

Helpful Tips

- **Saving:** Build an emergency fund and reach your goals.
- **Spending:** Cover needs and enjoy life—be smart!
- **Giving:** Help others and make a difference.
- **Growing:** Invest in your future to build wealth.

Good budgeting is about balance, not perfection. Adjust as you learn and grow!

Example: One Way to Divide $50

Category	Amount	Percent	What It Means
Saving	$20.00	40%	Builds security
Spending	$15.00	30%	Covers needs & wants
Giving	$5.00	10%	Helps others
Growing	$10.00	20%	Invests in the future
Total	**$50.00**	**100%**	

Plan your money. Protect your future. Make your dreams possible.

Money Math Practice

Instructions

Mateo earns $60 and saves 25%.
He also gives 10%.

Reflection Questions

- How much money does Mateo save?
- How much remains after savings?
- How much does he give?
- After saving and giving, how much spending money remains?

Bonus Challenge

If Mateo repeats this weekly for 8 weeks,
how much total will he save?

Budget Breakdown

Category	Amount	Percent	What It Means
Save	________	25%	Future goals
Give	________	10%	Helping others
Spend	________	Remaining %	Daily spending

Think About It

When you save consistently, small choices today can create bigger opportunities tomorrow.

Challenge Yourself

What would happen if Mateo saved 30% instead?

Small smart choices build big futures.

Where Does My Money Go?

Every dollar you spend is a choice. Make choices that build your future and support your **dreams!**

Money Tip: Your money has a job to do! Plan it. Spend it wisely. Save for tomorrow. Small choices today = big opportunities tomorrow!

Instructions

Think honestly about your current money habits.

Reflection Questions

- What do I spend the most money on?
- Do I save regularly?
- Do I spend emotionally?

Bonus Challenge

Financial confidence often begins with awareness.

Track Your Spending for 3 Days

Write down everything you spend money on for three days. Be honest—big or small, it all counts!

Day	What I Spent On	Amount ($)	Need or Want?	How I Felt
DAY 1	______	$______	☐ Need ☐ Want	🙂 😐 ☹️
DAY 2	______	$______	☐ Need ☐ Want	🙂 😐 ☹️
DAY 3	______	$______	☐ Need ☐ Want	🙂 😐 ☹️

Let's Reflect

What surprised me most? ______

- What are some things I can spend less on? ______
- What are some things I want to spend more on (because they help me grow or reach my goals)? ______

Smart Money Tip

Track → Review → Adjust

When you understand your spending, you can make better choices for your future!

Awareness is the first step. **Action** creates change. **You've got this!**

What Would You Do?

Great leaders make smart choices, even when it's not easy!

Emotional Spending

You had a stressful day and suddenly want to buy something online to feel better. The item looks fun, but you know you were saving your money for something important.

What would you do?

- ☐ Buy it immediately because you had a hard day
- ☐ Wait 24 hours before deciding
- ☐ Talk to someone you trust first
- ☐ Find another way to feel better without spending money

"Feelings come and go, but money choices can last a long time. Pause today, profit tomorrow."

– Smart Money Mindset

Tips to Handle Emotional Spending

Pause and Breathe – Take a deep breath. Give yourself a moment to calm down.

Use the 24-Hour Rule – Wait 24 hours before deciding. You may not want it tomorrow.

Talk About It – Share how you feel with someone you trust. It helps!

Remember Your Goals – Think about what you're saving for and why it matters.

Find Healthy Ways to Feel Better – Go for a walk, listen to music, read, draw, or spend time with people who make you happy.

Why It Matters!

Emotional spending can feel good for a moment, but it may lead to regret later. Strong leaders manage their feelings and make choices that support their future goals.

Self-control today leads to success tomorrow!

Think. | Plan. | Choose Wisely. | Build Your Future!

FUTURE CEO CHALLENGE: ONE-WEEK BUDGET PLAN

INSTRUCTIONS

Create a realistic budget for one full week.

REFLECTION QUESTIONS

- What is my weekly income?
- What is my savings goal?
- How will I spend, give, and grow money?

BONUS CHALLENGE

Strong businesses and strong futures both require planning.

STEP 1: SET YOUR INCOME & GOALS

MY WEEKLY INCOME

$ ____________

MY SAVINGS GOAL FOR THE WEEK

$ ____________

SMART GOALS

- **S** – Specific
- **M** – Measurable
- **A** – Achievable
- **R** – Relevant
- **T** – Time-bound

STEP 2: PLAN YOUR WEEK

Category	Purpose	Plan ($)	Actual ($)	Did I Stick to My Plan? ✓ or ✗
SAVE	Saving for goals (emergency fund, big purchase, etc.)	$ ________	$ ________	☐ Yes ☐ No
GIVE	Helping others (charity, donations, gifts)	$ ________	$ ________	☐ Yes ☐ No
SPEND	Needs & wants (food, fun, school, personal items)	$ ________	$ ________	☐ Yes ☐ No
GROW	Investing in yourself (education, skills, hobbies)	$ ________	$ ________	☐ Yes ☐ No
TOTAL		$ ________	$ ________	

STEP 3: REVIEW & REFLECT

- What went well this week? ____________________________
- What could I improve next week? ____________________________
- How did I do with my savings goal? ____________________________

MONEY MINDSET

- ☑ Plan ahead.
- ☑ Make smart choices.
- ☑ Avoid impulse spending.
- ☑ Stay consistent.
- ☑ Build my future!

> "A budget is telling your money where to go instead of wondering where it went."

Good money habits today build a better life tomorrow!

Chapter 2 Recap:
The Budget Blueprint

In this chapter, Maya and Mateo learned important real–world money lessons.

Budgeting Creates Freedom

A plan for your money gives you choices and peace of mind.

Small Habits Shape Bigger Outcomes

Little daily choices lead to big results over time.

Saving Protects Dreams

Saving today helps you be ready for tomorrow.

Giving Builds Character

Giving back helps others and makes you a better leader.

Growing Money Builds Future Opportunities

Investing in yourself and your goals creates more possibilities.

Financial Confidence Comes From Planning

When you plan your money, you believe in your future.

Final Chapter Message

A budget is more than numbers.

It is a roadmap for your future.

Pro Tips for Smart Money Moves

- ✔ Track your money so you know where it goes.
- ✔ Spend on things that matter most.
- ✔ Save first, spend second.
- ✔ Give with a grateful heart.
- ✔ Invest in learning new skills.
- ✔ Review your plan and adjust as you grow.

You don't have to be perfect—just be consistent and committed!

My Takeaway

The biggest lesson I learned in this chapter is...

____

____

One thing I will do differently with my money is...

____

____

I am most excited about...

____

____

Think About It

- What was the most important lesson in this chapter?

____

- How has your thinking about money changed?

____

- What will you do differently next time you feel pressured?

____

Smart habits today create powerful futures.

Smart shoppers compare before they buy!

SMART SHOPPING

Learning how to spend wisely, compare value, and avoid costly mistakes.

Smart shopping is not simply about buying less. It is about making thoughtful purchasing decisions that protect your future goals.

As Maya and Mateo begin exploring real-world spending, they discover that trends, sales, and social pressure can influence buying decisions. Learning to pause, compare, and think critically helps protect both confidence and future financial success.

KEY SHOPPING CHALLENGES

- Sales
- Trends
- Discounts
- Brand pressure
- Online ads
- Social influence

SMART SHOPPERS ASK:

- Is this a need or a want?
- Am I buying because of pressure?
- Is this the best value?
- Will this choice help or hurt my goals?

MY TAKEAWAY

The biggest lesson I learned in this chapter is...

____

____

One thing I will do differently with my money is...

____

____

I am most excited about...

____

____

THINK ABOUT IT

- What was the most important lesson in this chapter?

____

- How has your thinking about money changed?

____

- What will you do differently next time you feel pressured?

____

CHAPTER GOAL

This chapter helps students understand how advertising, emotions, and social pressure can influence spending decisions while building stronger consumer confidence.

Spend wisely. Choose value. Protect your future.

Think first, buy second, feel good later!

Story

The following weekend, Maya went shopping with friends. Bright sales signs covered every store window: 50% off, limited time, trending now.

Maya almost grabbed the first thing she saw, but then she paused.

She remembered her goal to save for her dream trip and asked herself, **"Do I really need this?"**

Instead of rushing, she compared prices, checked the quality, and chose the items that gave her the best value.

When the day was over, Maya felt proud. She had fun, stayed within her budget, and made choices that supported her future goals.

Lesson Embedded

Sales can feel urgent, but urgency does not always equal value.

Why It Matters

Understanding marketing tricks helps you make smarter money decisions and protect your future.

Key Takeaway

Smart shoppers pause before purchasing.

Think About It

- What helped Maya make a smart choice?
- How can you pause before a purchase?
- What is one goal you are saving for?

Plan smart. Spend smart. Succeed.

Story

Value lasts longer than trends!

Mateo studied two backpacks. One was trendy and expensive. The other was durable, practical, and less expensive.

"A sale is only a good deal if you actually need it," Mateo said.

He thought about how often he would use the backpack, how long it would last, and how it fit his needs.

Mateo chose the backpack that would last the whole year and help him stay organized, without draining his savings.

He felt confident knowing he made a smart choice based on value, not just the price tag.

Key Takeaway

Value includes usefulness, quality, and long-term benefit.

Why It Matters

Choosing value over trends helps you save money, reduce stress, and reach your goals faster.

Value vs. Price

Price is what you pay.
Value is what you get.

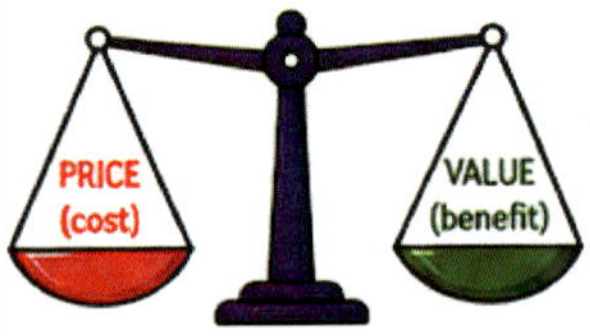

- ✓ A higher price does not always mean better value.
- ✓ Think about how long the item will last.
- ✓ Consider how it will help you every day.
- ✓ Look for quality, not just a big discount.

Think About It

- How did Mateo decide which backpack was the better choice?

  ____
- What does "value" mean to you?

  ____
- What are some things you can do to make smart choices like Mateo?

  ____

Real-World Tips

- ✓ Make a list before you shop.
- ✓ Compare options.
- ✓ Check reviews and ratings.
- ✓ Ask yourself: Do I really need it?
- ✓ Choose items that last and add value to your life.
- ✓ Avoid impulse purchases!

Smart Buying Checklist

1. Identify your need. What do you really need?
2. Research your options. Compare features, quality, and price.
3. Evaluate value. Think long-term benefits.
4. Decide wisely. Choose the option that gives more value.
5. Save & Succeed! Smart choices today lead to a better future.

Choose value today. Enjoy benefits tomorrow.

Story

Pause, think, choose wisely—that's real power!

Instead of buying impulsively, Maya asked herself:

- Will I use this often?
- Is this high quality?
- Does this fit my budget?
- Is this helping or hurting my goals?

Walking away from pressure felt powerful.

She remembered her goal to save for her dream trip and decided to wait.

Later, she found what she needed on sale—and it fit her budget perfectly!

Maya felt proud knowing she made a choice that supported her future instead of just satisfying a moment.

The Power of Pausing

Taking time before you buy helps you:

- ✓ Avoid buyer's remorse
- ✓ Save money
- ✓ Make smarter choices
- ✓ Stay focused on your goals
- ✓ Feel more in control

TIP: Take 24 hours to decide on non–essential purchases.

Needs vs. Wants

Ask yourself:

NEED	WANT
Something you must have	Something you would like to have
Helps you live or learn	Adds fun or convenience
Important for now	Nice, but can wait
Examples: food, school supplies, clothes, medicine	Examples: latest gadgets, brand names, trends

Reflection Questions

- What questions helped Maya make a smart choice?

____

____

- How can walking away from pressure help you?

____

____

- What goal are you saving for right now?

____

✓ Make a list before you shop.
✓ Compare options.
✓ Check reviews and ratings.
✓ Ask yourself: Do I really need it?
✓ Choose items that last and add value to your life.
✓ Avoid impulse purchases!

Think before you buy. Save today. Achieve tomorrow.

Smart money habits today lead to more freedom tomorrow!

Story

Instead of buying impulsively, Maya asked herself:

- Will I use this often?
- Is this high quality?
- Does this fit my budget?
- Is this helping or hurting my goals?

Walking away from pressure felt powerful.

She remembered her goal to save for her dream trip and decided to wait.

Later, she found what she needed on sale—and it fit her budget perfectly!

Maya felt proud knowing she made a choice that supported her future instead of just satisfying a moment.

Remember This!

Just because everyone else is buying it doesn't mean it's the right choice for you.

You have the power to decide what's best for your goals.

Budgeting Boost

A simple budget helps you:

- ✓ Track your money
- ✓ Plan for the things you want
- ✓ Avoid running out of money
- ✓ Reach your goals faster!

Confidence Builder

Every time you make a smart choice, you build your confidence and take control of your future.

You've got this!

PRO TIP

Delay today, enjoy tomorrow!

Waiting now can lead to bigger experiences, less stress, and more freedom later.

Big dreams start with small, smart choices.

Your future self will thank you for the choices you make today!

Strong choices today. More freedom tomorrow.

Every dollar you save today is a step closer to your dreams!

Maya's Mistakes:
Impulse Can Be Expensive

Maya remembered cheap accessories that broke, trendy items she stopped using, and snacks she did not really need. At first those purchases felt harmless, but over time they added up.

- ✗ Overspending
- ✗ Regret
- ✗ Delayed savings goals
- ✗ Financial stress
- ✗ Poor habits

What Impulse Buying Really Costs

Those small, unplanned purchases can have big consequences:

- Less money for the things that really matter.
- Feelings of regret and guilt.
- Harder to reach your savings goals.
- More stress and worry.
- Hard habits are tough to break.

Use the 5-Question Check

Before you buy, pause and ask:

1. Do I really need this?
2. Will I use this often?
3. Is this good quality?
4. Does this fit my budget?
5. Will this help me reach my goals?

Tips for Smarter Spending

- ✓ Make a budget and stick to it.
- ✓ Track your spending so you know where your money goes.
- ✓ Use cash or a debit card to avoid overspending.
- ✓ Wait before you buy—cooling off helps you think clearly.
- ✓ Save first, spend second.
- ✓ Celebrate progress, not just purchases!

DREAM FUND

Think before you buy. Save with purpose. Live your dreams.

Vocabulary Builder

Price	The amount of money you pay for something.
Value	The usefulness, benefits, and worth of something.
Quality	How well something is made or how well it works and lasts.
Discount	A decrease in price offered on an item.
Reduced Price	A lower price than the original price.
Impulse Buy	A purchase made quickly without careful thought or planning.
Bonus Tip	Words have power! The more you understand about money, the better choices you'll make.

Remember!

- Learn new words to build smart habits.
- Understand value, not just price.
- Take time to think before you buy.
- Look for quality that lasts, not just trends.
- Good choices today lead to a better future!

Compare Before You Buy

Instructions

Compare two products before making a decision.

- Product A price: $__________
- Quality: High / Medium / Low
- Need or Want?
- Product B price: $__________
- Quality: High / Medium / Low
- Need or Want?

Feature	Product A	Product B
Price How much will it cost you?		
Quality How well is it made? (High / Medium / Low)		
Need or Want? Is it something you really need?		
Benefits What's good about it?		
Drawbacks What's not so good?		
Overall Value Better / Same / Not as Good		

Quick Tips for Comparing

- Look beyond price. Consider quality, use, and value.
- Make a list of what matters most to you.
- Think about the long-term cost, not just now.
- The best choice today can help you save tomorrow.
- Choose what fits your needs and your goals.

Bonus Challenge

Good shoppers compare more than price. They compare value.

Compare wisely. Spend smarter. Build your future.

Don't let a good deal trick you into a bad decision!

Sale or Trap?

Decide if each scenario is a smart purchase or an unnecessary expense.

- ☆ Buy one, get one free candy
- ☆ 30% off shoes you do not need
- ☆ Discounted school supplies
- ☆ Popular hoodie on sale
- ☆ New phone accessory trend

Scenario	Smart Purchase (✓)	Unnecessary Expense (✗)	Why? Explain your choice.
1. Buy one, get one free candy	☐	☐	______
2. 30% off shoes you do not need	☐	☐	______
3. Discounted school supplies	☐	☐	______
4. Popular hoodie on sale	☐	☐	______
5. New phone accessory trend	☐	☐	______
Your own example: ______	☐	☐	______

Reflection Questions

- Do I need this? ______
- Is this helping my goals? ______
- Am I buying because of pressure? ______

Think Before You Buy, Compare Before You Commit. Choose What's Best for You!

Money Math Practice

Problem

A hoodie costs $40.
It is 25% off.
Sales tax is 8%.

Solve It Step by Step

1	Original Price	$40.00
2	Discount (25% off)	$________
3	Sale Price (after discount)	$________
4	Sales Tax (8% of sale price)	$________
5	Final Total (sale price + tax)	$________

Helpful Tips

- To find 25%: Multiply by 0.25
- To find 8%: Multiply by 0.08
- Add the sale price and tax to find the final total.

Quick Reminder

Discount lowers the price.
Sales tax adds to the price.
Always check the final total!

Original Price − Discount = Sale Price + Sales Tax = Final Total

Smart Math Tips

- Always calculate the real final price.
- Discounts lower the price before tax.
- Sales tax is added after discounts.
- Compare prices before buying.
- Waiting can help you save money.
- Smart shoppers focus on value, not pressure.

Smart math today builds smarter choices tomorrow.

Buy with purpose today, not impulse. Your future self will thank you!

Have You Ever Regretted a Purchase?

Think about an impulse purchase.

An impulse purchase is something you buy quickly without planning or thinking about if you really need it.

Why Do We Regret?

- We didn't really need it.
- We were influenced by ads, friends, or emotions.
- We didn't think about the consequences.
- It didn't bring lasting happiness.

Reflection Questions

1. What happened afterward?

   ____

   ____

2. Did the purchase truly make you happy?

   ____

   ____

3. What would you do differently now?

   ____

   ____

Learning from the past helps you make smarter choices today!

Tips to Avoid Regret

Pause Before You Buy
Take a moment. Don't let impulse decide for you.

Ask the Right Questions
Do I need this? Will I still want this next week or next month?

Use the 24-Hour Rule
Wait 24 hours before buying. You might change your mind!

Think About Your Goals
Will this purchase help or hurt your financial future?

Choose Value, Not Hype
Focus on what matters most, not what's popular.

Smart Shopper Advice

Regret gives us a lesson. A lesson helps us grow.
Grow stronger. Spend wiser. Build your future.

Think before you buy. Save today. Protect tomorrow.

Money choices today build the freedom of tomorrow!

What Would You Do?

You find a trendy product your friends love. A second option costs less, lasts longer, and has better quality.

TRENDY OPTION	SMARTER OPTION

Price: $89.99	Price: $39.99
Popular right now	Great quality
May break easily	Lasts longer
Shorter battery life	Better for your money

VS.

Reflection Questions

1. Which would you choose? Why?

____

____

2. How does popularity differ from value?

____

____

3. How can smart shopping protect future goals?

____

____

Smart shoppers think beyond today.
You can always make a wise choice!

Make a Smart Choice

Think Before You Buy
Take a moment. Ask if you really need it.

Compare Value
Look at price, quality, and how long it will last.

Think About the Future
Will this choice help you reach your goals?

Choose What Matters Most
Pick what gives you the best value, not just what's popular.

Remember:
Friends may come and go, but good habits and smart choices stay with you forever.

My Goals
- ☑ Save Money
- ☑ Buy What Matters
- ☑ Build My Future

Choose Value. Save Today. Achieve Tomorrow.

Every smart choice today builds a better future!

Chapter 3
Recap

In this chapter, you learned how to spend wisely, compare value, and avoid costly mistakes. **Let's review** what matters most!

1. Spend Wisely

- Make thoughtful choices, not impulse decisions.
- Pause, plan, and think before you buy.

2. Choose Value

- Look beyond price.
- Compare quality, longevity, and benefits.
- Choose what gives you the best value.

3. Protect Your Future

- Smart money choices help you reach your goals.
- Build good habits now for a stronger future.

Quick Self-Check

- I think before I buy.
- I compare my options.
- I choose value, not hype.
- I protect my future goals.
- I build smart money habits!

Money Mindset

Change the way you think about money, and you'll change your future.

- I am in control of my choices.
- I learn from my mistakes.
- I grow with every decision.

Action Step

Choose one smart shopping habit from this chapter. Practice it this week!

My habit goal:

Real-Life Scenario

You want a $60 hoodie because everyone at school has it.

But you find a hoodie for $35 that is better quality and will last longer.

What would you do?

- ☐ Buy the $60 hoodie to fit in.
- ☐ Buy the $35 hoodie for better value.
- ☐ Wait and save for something even better.

Extra Advice

Small choices may seem insignificant now, but they add up to BIG results over time!

Smart Choices Today. Better Habits Tomorrow. Stronger You!

Your talents today can build your future tomorrow!

Chapter 4
Earning Money

Learning how your skills, time, and creativity can create income.

Saving and budgeting are powerful, but earning money creates even more opportunities.

Ways to Earn Money

- Tutoring
- Yard Work
- Photography
- Creative Projects
- Pet Sitting
- Baking & Treats
- Digital Design
- Bookmarks
- Study Guides
- Seasonal Help

...and more!

What You Need

- **Skills:** What are you good at?
- **Time:** When are you available?
- **Responsibility:** Can people trust you?
- **Problem-solving:** Can you find solutions?
- **Helping others:** How can you make a difference?
- **Creativity:** Can you bring ideas to life?
- **Communication:** Can you listen and be clear?

Tips for Success

- Start small and stay consistent.
- Do your best in everything.
- Communicate clearly.
- Deliver quality work.
- Be dependable and honest.
- Save your earnings.
- Learn from mistakes.
- Keep improving every day!

Why It Matters

- Builds independence.
- Grows confidence.
- Creates opportunities.
- Teaches responsibility.
- Strengthens leadership.
- Builds future wealth.

Money Building Habits

- Tracks your earnings.
- Save a portion first.
- Reinvest in your growth.
- Build a good reputation.
- Practice consistency.

Chapter Goal

This chapter helps students understand how their unique abilities, creativity, and effort can become real-world income and future opportunities.

Real-Life Scenario

Maya designs birthday invitations because she loves art. People start asking her to make some for them.

What could she do next?

- ☐ Sell templates online.
- ☐ Offer custom designs.
- ☐ Build a portfolio.
- ☐ Save her profits.
- ☐ Expand her services.

Extra Advice

Look for everyday problems you can solve.

The best businesses often begin by helping others.

Future Entrepreneur Mindset

- I can create value.
- My ideas matter.
- Small steps lead to success.
- Practice builds mastery.

Try This!

List 3 skills you can use to earn money. Circle one you can use right away!

1. ____________
2. ____________
3. ____________

Every idea today can become income tomorrow!

Story

Mateo wanted more than allowance. He wanted independence and bigger goals. At the kitchen table, he wrote ideas: tutoring, selling bookmarks, organizing study kits, helping neighbors, and creative school supplies.

Lesson Embedded

Income often begins when skills create value.

Helpful Reminders

- Start with what you already know.
- Use your free time wisely.
- Ask for help and learn from others.
- Be reliable and keep your promises.
- Every small step leads to big results.

Types of Income

Active Income: You trade your time for money.

Passive Income: You earn money over time.

Side Income: Extra money from your skills or hobbies.

Success Tips

- Set a goal for what you want to earn.
- Make a simple plan.
- Take action, even if it's small.
- Learn from mistakes.
- Celebrate your progress!

Dream big, make a plan, and let your choices lead you there!

Story

As Maya and Mateo moved deeper into middle school, they realized that money plays a huge role in everyday life.

From buying lunch and school supplies to joining activities and planning for the future, they saw how money choices can affect their confidence, opportunities, and independence.

Through chores, small jobs, and side projects, they discovered that hard work builds more than cash—it builds character, discipline, and self-respect.

Together, they learned that understanding money early helps them make smarter decisions, build strong habits, and create a future full of freedom and success.

Smart Habits

- Track your spending.
- Save a portion of what you earn.
- Set short-term and long-term goals.
- Keep learning about money every day.

Ways to Earn

- Do chores or tasks for family.
- Offer services like babysitting or tutoring.
- Sell crafts, art, or digital products.
- Help with small jobs in your community.

What to Avoid

- Impulse spending.
- Keeping up with others.
- Ignoring your budget or goals.
- Thinking money will always be there.

Pro Tip!

The habits you build in middle school become the foundation for your freedom, success, and peace of mind in the future!

Remember:
Skills + Action + Consistency = Financial Freedom

Your Future is Built
Every smart choice you make today brings you closer to the life you dream about!

Start small, learn big, and never stop growing!

Story

Mateo's first business idea was simple: custom study kits with flashcards, organizers, motivational notes, and homework trackers.

Students loved them. Teachers noticed too.

Maya wondered if she could do something like that.

What They Did

- Identified a need at school.
- Created a helpful product.
- Kept it simple and useful.
- Listened to feedback.
- Worked together as a team.

What They Learned

- Small ideas can solve big problems.
- People appreciate products that help.
- Hard work and creativity can lead to success.
- Confidence grows when you take action.

Money Moment

- They invested their savings to buy supplies.
- They priced their kits fairly.
- They tracked income and expenses.
- They learned that profit comes from value, not just money.

Pro Tip!

Start small, stay consistent, and keep improving. Great things grow from small beginnings!

Big Ideas Start Small!

You don't need a huge plan—just a helpful idea and the courage to try.

Keep learning, keep creating, and keep going!

Every skill you have can become income when you use it to help others!

Mateo's Money Move: Skills Create Income

Mateo learned that earning money isn't just about asking for allowance—it's about using skills to help others.

- What am I good at?
- What problems can I solve?
- Who do I know I can help?
- How can I start?

He thinks about opportunities in his school and community where organization, creativity, helping others, and reliability are needed. Skills like planning, designing, tutoring, and organizing can become income.

Maya realized that learning money was not only about saving cash—but building confidence, creativity, and using skills wisely.

Together, they discovered that small actions with their skills can turn ideas into income that builds success.

Turning Skills Into Income

1. Identify your strengths
2. Notice real needs
3. Offer practical help
4. Start small
5. Improve your quality
6. Build trust

Mateo's Study Kit Success

Mateo's custom study kits included:

- Flashcards
- Motivational notes
- Organizational tools
- Homework trackers

How did students love them?

- Useful
- Organized
- Creative
- Unique

Builder Thinking

- Look for problems to solve.
- Use your skills.
- Help others.
- Start small and keep going.
- Keep learning every day!

Success Tips

- Practice your skills.
- Be reliable.
- Communicate clearly.
- Deliver quality work.
- Ask for feedback.
- Keep improving!

Next Steps

- Find one skill to use.
- Offer help this week.
- Track your results.
- Celebrate small wins.
- Dream bigger!

REMEMBER

Small ideas today can lead to big opportunities tomorrow!

Use Your Skills. Solve Problems. Build Your Future.

Different currencies, same value—money connects us all!

Vocabulary Builder

Understanding money words helps you make smart choices, grow confidence, and build stronger money habits.

	Income	Money earned or received.
	Skill	A talent or ability that creates value.
	Service	Helping others through useful work.
	Customer	A person who buys a product or service.
	Profit	Money left after expenses are paid.
	Responsibility	Managing tasks, money, and commitments wisely.
	Budget	A plan for how money will be earned, spent, or saved.
	Opportunity	A chance to create value or income.

Money Smart Tips

Read and Learn Daily
Read books, articles, and stories about money to grow your knowledge.

Use New Words
Practice using financial words in conversations and writing.

Ask Questions
Curiosity helps you understand money topics better.

Observe and Apply
Look for real-life examples and apply what you learn.

Teach Others
Explaining words to someone else helps you remember them.

Global Money Words

Financial literacy matters around the world.

United States	Dollar ($)
Japan	Yen (¥)
United Kingdom	Pound (£)
European Union	Euro (€)
Philippines	Peso (₱)

No matter where you travel, understanding money vocabulary helps you make smart choices **globally**.

Why This Matters

- Money skills work worldwide.
- Financial vocabulary builds confidence.
- Learning global currencies broadens understanding.
- Smart thinkers prepare for real-world opportunities.

Bonus Tip

Understanding vocabulary strengthens financial confidence and helps students think like future leaders.

Learn it. Use it. Apply it. Grow with it.

My Skills Can Earn

Instructions

List skills you already have.

- Drawing ____________
- Babysitting ____________
- Tutoring ____________
- Cleaning ____________
- Organizing ____________
- Writing ____________
- Crafting ____________

Reflection Questions

1. Which skills solve problems? ____
2. Which skills could earn income? ____
3. How could I improve these skills? ____

Bonus Challenge

Choose one skill and brainstorm one possible income idea.

My chosen skill: ____________________

How could I use this skill to help others?

____

____

____

My possible income idea:

Keep saving today for a better tomorrow!

My first income is the first step toward my big future!

My First Income Plan

Instructions

Create your first realistic earning idea.

- Business or Income Idea ____________________
- What problem does it solve? ____________________
- Who would benefit? ____________________
- Startup Cost $ __________
- Potential Weekly Earnings $ __________
- Savings Goal ____________________

Reflection Questions

- How would earning my own money strengthen my confidence?

____

____

Bonus Challenge

- Income can strengthen independence and self-belief.

The earlier you start saving, the more opportunities your future can bring!

Money Math Practice

Every time you sell something — like your art, notes, or extra school supplies — you turn effort into income!

Instructions

Mateo sells bookmarks for $3 each.

Supplies cost $12.

He sells 10 bookmarks.

Reflection Questions

- How much revenue did Mateo earn? ______________
- What were Mateo's costs? ______________
- What was Mateo's profit? ______________
- If he sells 20 bookmarks, what would his profit be? ______
- If Mateo saves 50% of his profit, how much would he save? ___

Bonus Challenge

If Mateo saves 50% of his profits, how much would he save?

Mateo would save $ ______

GREAT JOB!

Solve It Step by Step

1	How much revenue did Mateo earn? (Price × Quantity)	$ ______
2	What were Mateo's costs? (Supplies cost)	$ ______
3	What was Mateo's profit? (Revenue – Costs)	$ ______
4	If he sells 20 bookmarks, what would his profit be?	$ ______
5	If Mateo saves 50% of his profit, how much would he save?	$ ______
6	What is one smart choice Mateo could make with his savings?	______

Helpful Tips

- Revenue = Price × Quantity sold
- Profit = Revenue – Costs
- 50% means half (divide by 2)
- Good math = Smart money decisions!

Do the math. Make smart choices. Create your success!

Every dollar you earn is a step toward your dreams!

Building Confidence Through Earning

Instructions

Reflect on earning and responsibility.

Ways to Earn

(Ideas to Get You Started!)

- Offer to walk dogs or pet sit.
- Help with yard work or chores.
- Use your talents—art, music, or tutoring.
- Bake treats and sell them.
- Create digital designs, content, or crafts.
- Start a small business selling something handmade or helpful.

Money Confidence Tips

- Set a goal for what you want to save for.
- Track your earnings and spending.
- Save at least a part of what you earn.
- Be honest and reliable—it builds trust and more opportunities.
- Never stop learning—new skills can lead to more income!

Did You Know?

Many successful people started young by learning skills, solving problems, and taking small steps.

You can too!

Start Small
Dream Big
Keep Going

Think It Over!

Money doesn't just buy things—it gives you choices, freedom, and the power to help others.

Show Your Work!

Use this space to write your calculations or draw a plan.

Earn today. Learn always. Lead tomorrow.

Big ideas start small—your business can make a big difference!

Future CEO Challenge: Design Your First Safe Business

Instructions

Create a realistic business idea.

- Product or service ____________________
- Who it helps ____________________
- Startup cost ____________________
- Pricing ____________________
- Potential earnings ____________________
- Savings goal ____________________
- Marketing idea ____________________

My Business Idea

Use this space to describe your business and how it will be safe, helpful, and successful.

____

____

____

____

____

____

____

Reflection Questions

- What makes my idea safe and helpful?

____

____

____

Bonus Challenge

Create a business name and slogan.

Business Name: ____________________

Slogan: ____________________

____

CEO Success Tips

- Solve a real problem people face.
- Make sure your business idea is safe and legal.
- Keep your customers happy and treat them with respect.
- Track your money—know your income and expenses.
- Keep learning and ask for advice from trusted adults.
- Start small, stay consistent, and never give up!

CEO MINDSET

- ☑ Plan
- ☑ Work
- ☑ Learn
- ☑ Grow

Dream it. Plan it. Build it. Lead it. Make it matter!

Every lesson learned today is a step toward a brighter tomorrow! ♡

Chapter 4 Recap: Earning Money

In this chapter, Maya and Mateo learned important real-world money lessons.

- ☆ Skills can create income
- ☆ Creativity can solve problems
- ☆ Earning builds confidence
- ☆ Responsibility strengthens independence
- ☆ Small business ideas can grow
- ☆ Profit matters
- ☆ Leadership often begins with initiative

Key Takeaway

Earning money is more than making cash—it's about using your talents, making smart decisions, and creating value for others.

Smart choices today create a stronger future!

Final Chapter Message

Earning money is not only about income. It is about building freedom, confidence, and future possibilities.

What You Can Do Next

Set a Goal

Think about what you want to achieve and make a plan.

Keep Learning

Continue to build your skills and knowledge every day.

Help Others

Use what you learn to make a positive impact.

Take Action

Start small, stay consistent, and never stop growing!

"Your ideas have power. Your actions create change. Keep learning, keep earning, and keep leading!"

Chapter 5

Mini Business Builder

Big plans start with small steps and smart actions today!

Turning small ideas into bigger opportunities.

Entrepreneurship teaches students how to turn small ideas into bigger opportunities.

- Solving problems
- Creating products
- Offering services
- Understanding customers
- Leadership
- Communication
- Wealth-building

Design Goal

Maya and Mateo setting up a school event both with handmade products, flyers, price tags, customers, and a business notebook.

Skills You'll Build

- Creativity
- Planning
- Problem-solving
- Teamwork
- Money management
- Customer service
- Marketing basics

What You'll Do

- Brainstorm and choose a business idea.
- Make products or design services.
- Create flyers and promote your event.
- Set prices and track your sales.
- Learn from your customers and grow.

Chapter Goal

This chapter helps students understand how planning, creativity, and hard work can turn small ideas into successful mini businesses that build confidence and open doors to bigger opportunities.

"Small ideas can spark big change.
Plan it. Build it. Believe in it. Make it happen!"

Teamwork turns ideas into impact!

Story

Mateo's study kit business was growing. Maya wanted to join him. Together, they brainstormed handmade bookmarks, study kits, cultural crafts, baked goods, and school planners. Business was more than selling. It was creativity, planning, value, and leadership.

Lesson Embedded

Entrepreneurship combines creativity with strategy.

Key Takeaways

- Great ideas start small.
- Planning turns ideas into action.
- Teamwork makes business stronger.
- Creativity adds value.
- Leadership inspires others.

What They Learned

- How to identify products and services people need
- The importance of planning and organizing
- How to create value through creativity
- How teamwork and leadership drive success
- That every small step builds a bigger future

Words to Remember

Idea + Plan + Action
=
Opportunity

"Dream it. Plan it. Do it together.
Small steps today, big success tomorrow!"

Big businesses grow from smart planning!

Story

Lolo asked them important questions:

- What problem does your product solve?
- Who needs it?
- How much will supplies cost?
- What price creates profit?
- How will people learn about it?

Main Lesson

Business success depends on preparation, smart pricing, and solving real problems.

Maya realized successful businesses require planning, smart choices, and preparation before launching.

Questions Smart CEOs Ask

- What do people need?
- Can I afford supplies?
- Will I earn profit?
- How will customers find me?
- Is my product helpful?

Business Builder Tips

- Start small.
- Plan carefully.
- Know your costs.
- Price wisely.
- Stay organized.

Lolo's Wisdom

Planning today prevents mistakes tomorrow.

What They Learned

- Business planning builds confidence.
- Good pricing protects profit.
- Marketing helps customers find you.
- Preparation builds stronger success.
- Smart leaders think ahead.

Plan smart. Build wisely. Lead your future.

Creative ideas grow stronger with smart planning!

Story

Maya wanted things to look exciting.
Mateo focused on numbers.
Lolo reminded them both that successful businesses need creativity, planning, structure, and teamwork.

Together, they discovered that strong businesses balance imagination with organization.

Key Takeaway

Strong businesses combine innovation, planning, and organization.

Creative Business Skills

- Product design
- Marketing
- Branding
- Customer appeal
- Visual presentation

Smart Structure Skills

- Budgeting
- Inventory tracking
- Pricing
- Profit planning
- Organization

Lolo's Leadership Advice

Big dreams succeed when creativity meets preparation.

What Maya and Mateo Learned

- Creativity attracts attention.
- Organization protects profit.
- Teamwork builds stronger ideas.
- Planning reduces mistakes.
- Leadership requires balance.

Your Business Balance Plan

My creative idea: ______________________

My product: ______________________

My target customer: ______________________

My budget plan: ______________________

My pricing goal: ______________________

Create boldly. Plan wisely. Build successfully.

Your business can change lives–including your own!

Lolo's Legacy Lesson: Business Builds More Than Profit

"Businesses do more than make money," Lolo said. "They create solutions, leadership, discipline, responsibility, financial opportunity, and confidence."

Key Lesson

Business ownership builds financial and personal growth.

What Business Builds

- Problem solving
- Leadership skills
- Discipline and focus
- Financial opportunity
- Confidence and purpose

Life Skills You Gain

- Communication
- Decision making
- Time management
- Money management
- Responsibility

Lolo's Wisdom

A business is not just about profit.
It's about creating value that lasts.

Remember This

- Help people
- Solve problems
- Build trust
- Create value
- Leave a legacy

Daily Actions to Build a Better Business

Think Big
Dream of how your business can help others and improve your community.

Plan Smart
Set goals, make a plan, and use your time wisely.

Manage Well
Track your money, control costs, and save for growth.

Communicate Clearly
Share your ideas, listen to feedback, and build relationships.

Use your success to support others and create a positive impact.

Success Tip
Small actions today build a stronger business tomorrow.

Build a business. | Build a future. | Build a legacy.

Big words today, big success tomorrow!

Vocabulary Builder

Business	An organization or activity that sells products or services.
Product	An item created for sale.
Service	Helpful work offered to others.
Startup Cost	The money needed to begin a business.
Revenue	Total money earned before expenses.
Profit	Money remaining after expenses are removed.

Remember:

Strong words build strong ideas—and strong ideas build strong businesses!

Cool Facts to Know!

Many big companies started small! Amazon began in a garage. Apple started in a home.

Ideas become businesses when people solve problems for others.

Revenue grows when customers trust your product or service.

Watching expenses carefully helps profits grow stronger.

Businesses that care about people and the planet create a better future for all.

Teamwork, honesty, and kindness are the secret ingredients to lasting success.

Words have power.

The more you understand, the more confident you become. Keep building your vocabulary, and you'll build your future!

Why Vocabulary Matters

- Helps you understand big ideas.
- Improves reading and writing.
- Builds confidence in speaking.
- Prepares you for future success.

Growth Mindset

- Mistakes help you learn.
- Challenges help you grow.
- Effort today leads to success tomorrow!

Think Like an Entrepreneur

- Be curious.
- Ask questions.
- Find a need.
- Create a solution.
- Make a positive impact.

Do the math. Make smart choices. Build a better future!

Great ideas start small, but smart planning makes them grow big!

Build My Business Idea

Instructions

Create your own mini business plan.

1. Business Name: ____________________
2. Product or Service: ____________________
3. Who needs it? ____________________
4. What problem does it solve? ____________
5. Startup Cost: $____________
6. Selling Price: $____________
7. Profit Goal: $____________

Business Idea Checklist

- ☑ Solves a real problem
- ☑ People will buy it
- ☑ I can afford to start
- ☑ I can make a profit
- ☑ I am excited about it!

Plan for Success

- Know your customers.
- Keep your costs low.
- Offer great value.
- Market your idea.
- Keep learning and improving.

Reflection Questions

- Why would someone buy this?

____

____

- How will my business help others?

____

____

Bonus Challenge

Design a logo or slogan for your business.

____

My Business Idea in One Sentence

My business will ____________________

____

Plan smart. Build wisely. Lead your future.

Track how your business earns money!

Profit Tracker

Instructions

Use this page to track your income, expenses, and profit. The more you track, the more you grow!

1. Supplies Cost
(What did it cost to make or buy your product?)
$ ________

2. Price Per Item
(How much do you sell each item for?)
$ ________

3. Number Sold
(How many items did you sell?)
____

4. Total Revenue
(Price per item × Number sold)
$ ________

5. Total Profit
(Total Revenue – Supplies Cost)
$ ________

Plan to Grow

- ☑ Lower my costs
- ☑ Raise my prices wisely
- ☑ Sell to more people
- ☑ Improve my product
- ☑ Track my results

Quick Tip

Profit = Money you keep after paying for what you need to run your business.

Reflection Questions

- Is my pricing effective?
____
____
- How can I increase profits?
____
____

Bonus Challenge

If you could double your profit next month, what would you do differently?
____
____
____

My Goal in One Sentence

This month, I will ________
____

Small steps today. Big success tomorrow.

Know Your Customer

Instructions

Think carefully about your target audience.

Reflection Questions

- Who is most likely to buy my product?
- Why do they need it?
- What problem am I solving?
- How can I improve my offer?

Why It Matters

- Happy customers come back.
- Understanding customers helps you sell more.
- Solve real problems and people will support you.
- Great businesses start with knowing their customers.

Bonus Challenge

Customer understanding strengthens business growth.

Create a Customer Profile

Describe your ideal customer.

Age ____________________

Gender ____________________

Interests ____________________

Needs ____________________

Challenges ____________________

Where do they spend time? ____________________

What matters most to them? ____________________

Ways to Learn About Customers

- Ask questions and listen to answers.
- Create simple surveys.
- Check social media and online reviews.
- Talk to people face-to-face.
- Pay attention to what customers like and don't like.

Money Tip

Focus on value, not just price. Happy customers are worth more than a quick sale!

Example: Homemade Soap Business

Who are they?	Why do they need it?	Problem I solve	How I improve my offer
Teens and adults who care about natural products.	They want healthy skin and eco-friendly choices.	I provide soaps that are natural, gentle, and good for the planet.	Offer new scents, pretty packaging, and great service!

Why Vocabulary Matters

- Helps you understand big ideas.
- Improves reading and writing.
- Builds confidence in speaking.
- Prepares you for future success.

Growth Mindset

Mistakes help you learn.
Challenges help you grow.
Effort today leads
to success tomorrow!

Think Like an Entrepreneur

- Be curious.
- Ask questions.
- Find a need.
- Create a solution.
- Make a positive impact.

Every customer you understand is a step closer to a successful business!

Every dollar has a job! Plan it, spend it, and grow it wisely.

Money Math Practice

Instructions

Maya spends $25 on supplies. She sells products for $5 each. She sells 15 products.

Math Tips

- Revenue = Price × Quantity
- Profit = Revenue – Expenses
- Reinvesting helps your business grow!
- Track your money to make smart choices.

Reflection Questions

- How much revenue did Maya earn?
- What was Maya's profit?
- If she reinvests $20, how much remains?

Bonus Challenge

Understanding reinvestment builds business intelligence.

Maya's Business Breakdown

Supplies Cost (Expenses)	$ ________
Price Per Product	$ ________
Number of Products Sold	________
Total Revenue (Price × Quantity)	$ ________
Total Profit (Revenue – Expenses)	$ ________
Reinvested Amount	$ ________
Amount Remaining	$ ________

More Practice

1. Liam spends $40 on supplies. He sells each item for $6. He sells 12 items. What is his profit?

   ____

2. Ava spends $30 on supplies. She sells each item for $7. She sells 10 items and reinvests $15. How much money does she have left?

   ____

3. Noah spends $50 on supplies. He sells each item for $8. He sells 20 items and reinvests $40. How much money does he have left?

   ____

Every dollar you save and invest today builds the success of tomorrow!

Great ideas solve problems, help people, and create a better future!

Future CEO Challenge: My First Business Pitch

Instructions

Write or present your business idea in **30 seconds.**

1. What you offer ______________________________
2. Who it helps ______________________________
3. Why it matters ______________________________
4. Pricing ______________________________
5. Why customers should choose you ______________________________

Pitch Like a Pro!

- Start strong – grab attention right away.
- Keep it simple – use short, clear sentences.
- Focus on the benefit, not just the product.
- Speak with confidence and smile!
- End with a powerful sentence or question.

30-Second Structure

0–5 sec	**Hook** Introduce your idea in one exciting line.
5–15 sec	**Explain** What you offer and who it helps.
15–25 sec	**Value** Why it matters and what makes it special.
25–30 sec	**Close** Why customers should choose you.

Reflection Question

- How can I speak clearly and confidently?

____

____

Great Pitches Have...

- A clear idea people understand.
- A purpose that solves a problem.
- Confidence and positive energy.
- A strong reason to believe.
- Trust and connection with others.
- A smart plan for growth and success.

Little ideas today can create big opportunities tomorrow!
Believe in yourself, take action, and make it happen!

Plan your dreams today, build your success tomorrow!

Vision Board:
My Future Business Goals

Instructions

Draw or map your future business goals.

- Dream business ____________
- Financial goals ____________
- Future lifestyle ____________
- Skills to improve ____________
- Leadership goals ____________

Vision Inspiration

- Dream big, but start small.
- Set clear goals and work toward them every day.
- Believe in your ideas and yourself.
- Stay focused, stay motivated, never give up!

Reflection Question

- How can today's habits shape tomorrow's opportunities?

____

____

Steps to Build Your Vision

1. Imagine your future. What does success look like?
2. Set your goals. Be specific and realistic.
3. Plan your actions. What steps will get you there?
4. Stay consistent. Small actions lead to big results.

Bonus Challenge

Create a visual collage or digital board that shows your business dreams. Share it with someone who encourages and inspires you!

Examples of Future Business Goals

My Business	Money Goals	Lifestyle Goals	Skills to Learn	Impact Goals
Start my own business that helps people.	Earn enough income to support my dream life.	Travel, spend time with family, and enjoy life.	Improve my marketing, sales, and leadership.	Make a positive difference in my community.

Dream it. Plan it. Do it together.
Small steps today, big success tomorrow!

Small steps today lead to big success tomorrow!

Reflection and Real-World Practice

Instructions

Think about how this chapter connects to your own life and future goals.

Reflection Questions

- What did I learn?
- What habit can I improve?
- How can this help my future?

____

____

____

____

Bonus Challenge

Apply one lesson this week.

Keep Dreaming
Big goals start with a vision.

Keep Learning
New skills create new opportunities.

Stay Focused
Distractions don't build your future.

Take Action
Small steps create big changes.

Believe in Yourself
You have the power to make it happen.

Never Give Up
Challenges help you grow stronger.

Your future is built by the choices you make today.
Spend your time, work hard, and watch your goals grow!

Think Big.
Start Small.
Keep Going.
Make It Happen!

Chapter 5 Recap:
Mini Business Builder

In this chapter, Maya and Mateo learned important real-world money lessons.

- Entrepreneurship begins with solving problems.
- Planning strengthens business success.
- Creativity builds opportunity.
- Profit matters.
- Leadership matters.
- Customer understanding matters.
- Public speaking strengthens growth.
- Vision strengthens future success.

Key Takeaway

Every great business starts with a purpose, a plan, and the courage to take action.

You have the power to build your own success story!

What You Can Do Next

- Keep learning about money and business.
- Practice your ideas and develop your skills.
- Stay curious and look for problems to solve.
- Work with others and lead with kindness.
- Take action—your future is in your hands!

Reflect and Grow

- What was your favorite lesson in this chapter?

____

____

- How will you use what you learned in your future?

____

____

Skills You Built in This Chapter

Problem Solving	Planning	Creativity	Money Management	Leadership	Communication	Public Speaking	Vision

"Small ideas can change everything. Keep learning, keep growing, keep believing!"

Good Banking Habits Today Lead to a Better Tomorrow!

Chapter 6

Banking Basics

Understanding how banks help protect, organize, and grow money.

Managing money wisely also means understanding financial systems. Banks can protect money, organize finances, track spending, build discipline, and prepare for larger goals.

What You'll Learn

- Savings accounts
- Deposits
- Withdrawals
- Balances
- Debit cards
- Interest
- Bank statements
- Organization

Why Banking Matters

- Keeps your money safe and secure.
- Helps you track and manage your money.
- Builds financial discipline and responsibility.
- Prepares you for big goals and opportunities.
- Encourages smart choices and independence.

Bank Services You Might Use

- Savings Accounts
- Deposits
- Withdrawals
- Check Balances
- Debit Cards
- Earn Interest
- Bank Statements
- Organize Finances

Chapter Goal

This chapter helps students understand the basic banking services and how using a bank wisely can protect money, support smart spending, and build a strong financial future.

Save smart. Bank smart. Grow strong.
Your future is in your hands!

Every dollar you spend is a vote for your future!

Story

One sunny Saturday, Maya and Mateo went to the mall with Lolo.

Maya spotted a new pair of designer sneakers. “They are so cool!” she said. “I really want them.”

Mateo looked at the price tag. “Whoa! That’s a lot of money. Is this a need or a want?”

Lolo smiled. “Great questions! Needs are things we must have to live or learn. Wants are things we would like to have, but we can live without.”

Maya thought for a moment. “I don’t need these sneakers. I already have shoes that work fine.”

Mateo added, “Let’s use our Smart Money Guide.”

They checked their savings goal for their business. “If we wait,” Maya said, “we can still get them later and keep working toward our bigger dream.”

They walked away feeling proud of their choice.

Key Lesson

Understanding the difference between needs and wants helps us make smart money choices that support our goals.

Key Takeaway

When we pause, think, and plan, we make choices that help us save, grow, and reach our dreams.

Reflection Question

- What is something you really want right now? Is it a need or a want? Why?

____

____

Life Skill Spotlight

Learning to pause and choose wisely builds confidence, discipline, and financial freedom.

Think before you spend. Choose what matters. Stay focused on your goals!

Good habits today create financial freedom tomorrow.

Story

Inside the bank, Maya and Mateo learned about savings accounts, deposits, withdrawals, debit cards, balances, and interest. The bank protected money, and helped build habits.

The teller explained, "A savings account is a safe place to keep your money. When you deposit money, you are saving it. When you withdraw money, you are taking some out."

Mateo asked, "What is interest?"

The teller smiled. "Interest is extra money you earn just for saving. The more you save, the more you can earn over time."

Maya said, "So, saving now can help us reach our big goals later!"

Lolo added, "Exactly! Banking gives you structure, and structure builds success."

Maya and Mateo left the bank excited and empowered to grow their future.

Key Banking Basics

Savings Account — A safe place to keep your money while you save for your goals.

Deposit — Putting money into your account to save for the future.

Withdrawal — Taking money out of your account when you need it.

Debit Card — A card you can use to pay for things using the money in your account.

Balance — The total amount of money in your account after deposits and withdrawals.

Interest — Extra money you earn for saving your money over time.

Why It Matters

- Keeps your money safe
- Helps you build good money habits
- Grows your money over time
- Supports your future goals

Think About It

What is one money habit you can start today to build a better future?

____

____

Life Skill Spotlight

Using a bank helps you practice responsibility, planning, and patience—skills that lead to lifelong success!

Discipline with money today, freedom in life tomorrow.

Small steps today lead to big possibilities tomorrow.

Story

Lolo explained, "A bank protects your money physically. But your habits protect your future financially."

Maya understood that strong money habits matter more than how much money you start with.

Mateo said, "So small choices today can lead to big results tomorrow?"

"Exactly!" Lolo replied.

"Every time you save, plan, or spend wisely—you are building the life you dream of."

Maya smiled. "Let's keep building our habits so we can build our future!"

They left the bank with new knowledge—and a new commitment to their goals.

Key Takeaway

Strong habits create stronger futures.

Habit Builder Challenge

Choose one money habit to focus on this week and take action!

- Save a little each day.
- Plan before you spend.
- Spend on things that matter.
- Stay consistent—don't give up!

Small actions today build the life you want tomorrow.

Goal Getter Corner

Think about your future!
What do you want to achieve?

- A new skill
- A dream trip
- Helping others
- Financial freedom

Your goals are possible when your habits are strong!

Build smart habits today, unlock amazing tomorrows.

Strong habits today, powerful choices tomorrow, a life of possibilities. ♡

Lolo's Legacy Lesson: Build Strong Money Habits Early

Banks can help you save safely, track spending, build discipline, prepare for emergencies, and strengthen independence.

THE STORY

- Lolo taught Maya and Mateo that banks protect money, while good habits build a better future.
- He showed them that small, consistent choices can lead to big results over time.
- They learned to start early, make smart choices, and use the right tools to reach their goals.
- Maya and Mateo left with a promise to build strong habits and create their best future.

BUILD GOOD HABITS EARLY

The earlier you build good money habits, the easier it becomes to reach your goals and create a better future for yourself.

USE THE RIGHT TOOLS

Banks, budgets, and saving plans are powerful tools that help protect your money and support your success.

MAKE SMART CHOICES

Every smart choice you make today brings you one step closer to the life you want tomorrow.

EXTRA TIPS TO SUCCEED

SET GOALS
Write down your goals and keep them in mind every day.

SAVE CONSISTENTLY
Save a little bit regularly, even if it's a small amount.

TRACK SPENDING
Know where your money goes so you can make better decisions.

KEEP LEARNING
The more you learn about money, the more confident and successful you'll be.

STAY DISCIPLINED
Good habits take time, but they build a strong future.

BUILD STRONG HABITS TODAY, AND YOUR FUTURE WILL THANK YOU.

Big steps today, brighter future!

Vocabulary Builder

Learn these important banking words to grow your money knowledge!

Bank	A financial institution that stores and manages money.
Deposit	Money added into an account.
Withdrawal	Money taken out of an account.
Balance	The amount of money currently in an account.
Debit Card	A card used to access money directly from your bank account.
Interest	Extra money earned or charged over time.

Bonus Tip: Understanding vocabulary strengthens financial confidence.

Put Your Knowledge to Work!

Write the correct vocabulary word next to each definition.

1. ______________________ Money added into an account.
2. ______________________ The amount of money currently in an account.
3. ______________________ A card used to access money from your bank account.
4. ______________________ Money taken out of an account.
5. ______________________ Extra money earned or charged over time.
6. ______________________ A financial institution that stores and manages money.

The more you learn today, the more your money can do for you tomorrow.

Save a little today, smile more tomorrow, live your best future.

My Bank Register

Instructions

Practice tracking money like a real bank account holder.

Account Summary

- Starting Balance $__________
- Deposit $__________
- Withdrawal $__________
- Remaining Balance $__________

Helpful Tip

Always check your balance so you know what you can spend, save, or plan for!

Date	Description	Deposit (+)	Withdrawal (−)	Balance (=)

Reflection Questions

- Did I track my money carefully?

____

____

- Why is knowing my balance important?

____

____

Bonus Challenge

Add multiple transactions.

- Make at least 3 deposits and 3 withdrawals.
- Track your balance after each transaction.
- What patterns do you notice?

____

____

"Track your money today, take control of your tomorrow."

Understand today, prepare better for tomorrow.

Reading My Bank Statement

Instructions

Review a sample bank statement and use it to answer the questions.

My Bank Statement

Account Holder: Jordan Lee

Account Number: 1234 5678 9012   Statement Period: May 1 – May 31, 2026

Starting Balance	Total Deposits	Total Withdrawals	Ending Balance
$250.00	$450.00	$230.00	$470.00

Date	Description	Deposits (+)	Withdrawals (−)	Balance
May 1	Starting Balance			$250.00
May 3	Deposit	$150.00		$400.00
May 8	Withdrawal – ATM		$60.00	$340.00
May 12	Deposit	$200.00		$540.00
May 15	Withdrawal – Groceries		$75.00	$465.00
May 20	Withdrawal – Online		$95.00	$370.00
May 25	Deposit	$100.00		$470.00
May 31	Ending Balance			$470.00

What Do These Terms Mean?

- **Starting Balance:** The amount of money in your account at the beginning of the statement period.
- **Deposit:** Money added to your account.
- **Withdrawal:** Money taken out of your account.
- **Ending Balance:** The amount of money in your account at the end of the statement period.

Helpful Tip

Review your bank statement each month to track your money, spot errors, and make smart decisions!

Reflection Questions

1. How much was deposited in total? ____________________
2. How much was withdrawn in total? ____________________
3. What is the final (ending) balance? ____________________
4. Were any purchases unnecessary? If yes, which ones? ____________________

   ____
5. How can reviewing your statement help you manage your money better?

   ____

   ____

"Financial knowledge today, financial freedom tomorrow."

Positive habits today lead to financial freedom tomorrow. ♡

Money Math Practice

Instructions

Solve the problems below using addition and subtraction. Show your work!

Money Tip

Track your money, set goals, and save a little at a time. It adds up!

Let's Practice! ♡

You start with $100.

- You deposit $30.
- You spend $25.

1. How much is your new balance? ____________
2. If you save $15 next week, what will your balance be? ________
3. How can consistent saving help? ____________________

____

____

Break It Down!

Starting amount	$100
+ Deposit	+ $30
= Subtotal	$130
− Spending	− $25
= New Balance	$105

Balance After Saving $15 Next Week

New Balance	$105
+ Next Week Savings	+ $15
= New Balance	$120

Every little bit moves you closer to your goals! ♡

Bonus Challenge

How much would your balance grow after 8 weeks of saving $15 each week?

Show your work.

____

____

____

Good money choices today build the life you want tomorrow. ♡

How Does Banking Build Confidence?

Money doesn't grow on trees. Good habits grow your future!

Instructions

Reflect on how banking and good habits help you feel more confident with money.

How Banking Helps

- Keeps your money safe.
- Helps you track spending.
- Makes saving easier.
- Builds good money habits.
- Prepares you for the future.

Habits That Build Confidence

- Track my money every day.
- Save a part of what I learn.
- Budget for needs and wants.
- Avoid wasteful spending.
- Learn and keep improving.

My Action Plan

1. One habit I will start: ____________________
2. One goal I will save for: ____________________
3. How I will stay organized: ____________________

   ____
4. How I will track my money: ____________________

   ____

More Money Tips

- **Read your bank statements.** Check each month to understand your money and catch any mistakes.
- **Avoid unnecessary fees.** Know your bank's rules to avoid extra charges like overdraft or ATM fees.
- **Set savings goals.** Having a goal, like a new bike or a trip, makes saving easier and more exciting.
- **Use digital tools.** Banking apps can help you track, budget, and save smarter.
- **Ask questions.** Don't be afraid to ask your bank or a trusted adult if you don't understand something.
- **Build an emergency fund.** Save a little at a time for surprises like repairs or unexpected experises.
- **Revisit your goals.** Check your goals often and adjust your plan as your needs change.

Extra Tips for Confidence

- Start small when saving. Every little bit counts!
- Be consistent. Small steps create big change.
- Keep your money information private and safe.
- Ask for help. Talk to a trusted adult.
- Celebrate progress. You're building a better future!

Confidence with money comes from good habits.
Keep learning, keep saving, keep growing!

Small decisions with money today can open big doors tomorrow.

What Would You Do?

Instructions

You receive $200 for your birthday!
Explore the choices below and decide what is best for your future.

You receive $200. What would you do?

1. Spend It Immediately

Buy something you want right now.

Examples:

- New clothes
- Gaming gear
- Gadgets

2. Save Part of It

Save some for later needs or goals.

Examples:

- Emergency fund
- Save for a bike
- Save for college

3. Deposit It in the Bank

Keep your money safe and earn interest.

Examples:

- Savings account
- Certificate of deposit (CD)
- Money market account

4. Invest in a Future Business Goal

Use the money to start or grow a business idea.

Examples:

- Buy supplies
- Create products
- Build your brand

Reflection Questions

1. Which choice supports long-term growth?

____

____

2. Why?

____

____

Compare the Choices

Write one short-term benefit and one long-term benefit for each choice.

Choice	Short-Term Benefit	Long-Term Benefit
1. Spend It		
2. Save Part		
3. Deposit It		
4. Invest It		

Money Tip

The 50/30/20 Rule can help you make smart choices:

50% Needs

30% Wants

20% Savings & Goals

Balance today, freedom tomorrow!

Bonus Challenge

Pretend you choose one option. Write a short plan for how you will use the $200 wisely.

My Choice: ____________________

My Plan: ____________________

____

MY PLAN

- ☐ What I will do
- ☐ How it helps me
- ☐ What I hope to achieve

The money you manage today is the freedom you enjoy tomorrow.

Chapter 6 Recap: Banking Basics

In this chapter, Maya and Mateo learned important real-world money lessoms.

Banks Protect Money

Banks keep your money safe and secure so you can focus on your goals.

Organization Builds Confidence

When you organize your money and time, you feel more in control and less stressed.

Deposits Grow Savings

Putting money in a savings account helps it grow over time with interest.

Tracking Spending Strengthens Habits

Tracking where your money goes helps you make better choices.

Discipline Matters

Sticking to good money habits today leads to better results tomorrow.

Financial Systems Create Structure

Systems like budgeting, saving, and banking help your money work for you.

Long-Term Planning Protects Goals

Planning ahead helps you reach your dreams and handle life's surprises.

Key Takeaways

- Keep your money safe in a bank.
- Save a part of what you earn.
- Track your spending.
- Make smart choices.
- Stay consistent.
- Plan for your future.

Why Banking Matters

Banks and banking tools help you:

- Keep your money safe.
- Earn interest on savings.
- Build good credit for the future.
- Access loans for big goals like college or a home.
- Learn responsibility and independence.
- Create a strong foundation for financial success.

More Money Tips

- **Read your statements.** Check your bank statement each month to understand your money and catch any mistakes.
- **Avoid unnecessary fees.** Know your bank's rules to avoid extra charges like overdraft or ATM fees.
- **Set savings goals.** Having a goal, like a new bike or a trip, makes saving easier and more exciting.
- **Use digital tools.** Banking apps can help you track, budget, and save smarter.
- **Ask questions.** Don't be afraid to ask your bank or a trusted adult if you don't understand something.
- **Build an emergency fund.** Save a little at a time for surprises like repairs or unexpected expenses.
- **Revisit your goals.** Check your goals often and adjust your plan as your needs change.

Smart choices today lead to stronger futures tomorrow.

Good money habits today lead to a stronger future.

Chapter 7

Credit and Borrowing Basics

Borrowing money can help you now, but understanding how it works keeps your future safe. Smart borrowing is about responsibility, planning, and good choices.

What Is Credit?

Credit is borrowed money that you agree to pay back later, usually with interest.

Examples:

- Credit cards
- Personal loans
- Student loans
- Buy now, pay later

Why It Matters

Using credit wisely can help you build trust with lenders and open doors to future opportunities.

Benefits:

- Build credit history
- Access to larger loans
- Financial independence
- Emergency help

Key Things to Understand

Borrow	Agree	Repay	Interest	Credit Score
You borrow money from a bank, lender, or company.	You agree to pay it back by a certain date with interest.	Make payments on time. Late payments can hurt your credit.	This is the extra cost for borrowing money.	Your payment history affects your score, which shows how reliable you are.

Smart Borrowing Tips

- Borrow only what you need.
- Understand the total cost.
- Always read the terms.
- Make payments on time.
- Avoid using all your credit.
- Build savings to avoid debt.

Reflection Questions

1. Why is it important to understand how credit works before borrowing?

____

____

2. How can borrowing help you reach your goals if used wisely?

____

____

Chapter Goal

This chapter helps students understand how outside pressure can influence spending and how true financial confidence begins with thoughtful decision-making.

Borrow with a plan. Repay with pride.
Build a future of choices, not regrets.

Think before you borrow. Plan before you pay.

Story

Maya noticed an online ad: Buy now. Pay later.
The offer seemed exciting.
But Lola explained that simple does not always mean safe. Borrowing can help when used wisely, but without understanding it can become expensive.

Lesson Embedded

Credit tools can feel easy but require responsibility.

What Maya Learned

- Borrowing is a promise to pay back.
- Interest makes borrowing cost more.
- Missing payments can hurt your credit.
- Smart choices today build a better tomorrow.

The Cost of Debt

- Interest makes items more expensive.
- Debt can cause stress and worry.
- It can hurt your credit score.
- Big debt can limit your future opportunities.
- It takes longer to reach your goals.

Think It Through

Before borrowing, ask yourself:

- Do I really need this?
- Can I afford the payments?
- Do I understand the total cost?
- What happens if I miss a payment?
- Is there a better option?

Reflection Questions

1. Why is it important to understand the full cost of borrowing money?

____

____

2. How can making payments on time help your future?

____

____

Real-World Connection

Adults use borrowing for many reasons—like cars, homes, or education. Understanding credit now helps you make smart choices and avoid costly mistakes later.

Use credit like a tool, not a shortcut.
Smart choices today build freedom tomorrow.

Discipline today keeps debt away and freedom closer tomorrow.

Story

Lola explained that credit means borrowing money. It is not free. If you do not repay it on time, interest adds up. Maya understood that debt could quietly grow if not managed responsibly.

Main Lesson

Debt grows when discipline is missing.

How Debt Grows

- You borrow money.
- Interest adds to what you owe.
- Miss a payment.
- Late fees are added.
- Your balance grows.
- It becomes harder to pay back.

The Cost of Debt

- Interest makes items more expensive.
- Debt can cause stress and worry.
- It can hurt your credit score.
- Big debt can limit your future opportunities.
- It takes longer to reach your goals.

Types of Debt

Good Debt

Helps you build a future and increase value, like a home loan or education loan.

Bad Debt

Used for things that lose value quickly, like luxury items you don't really need.

Secured Debt

Backed by something valuable, like a car loan or mortgage.

Unsecured Debt

Not backed by anything physical, like credit card balances or personal loans.

Student Debt

Money borrowed for education that must be repaid later.

Extra Tips for Confidence

- Even small steps make a big difference!
- Be consistent. Small steps create big change.
- Keep your money information private and safe.
- Ask for help. Talk to a trusted adult.
- Celebrate progress. You're building a better future!

Wise choices today keep debt away and your dreams within reach.

Story

Lola showed a simple example: If you borrow $200 and interest adds more, the purchase costs more than the original price. The difference depends on knowledge and discipline.

Small choices now can save you big money and stress later.

Key Takeaway

Patience often protects wealth.

Key Takeaway

Patience often protects wealth.

Why Interest Adds Up

- Interest is the extra cost of borrowing.
- It may be small at first but grows over time.
- The longer you take to repay, the more you pay.
- High interest can make debt hard to escape.

Simple Example

You borrow $200 at 10% interest for 1 year.

Interest = $200 × 10% = $20

Total to repay = $200 + $20

= **$220**

Lesson: It costs more than you borrowed.

Interest Over Time

Amount Borrowed	Interest Rate (Per Year)	Time	Interest Amount	Total to Repay
$200	5%	1 year	$10	$210
$200	10%	1 year	$20	$220
$200	10%	2 years	$44	$244
$200	15%	2 years	$66	$266

Smart Borrower's Checklist

- Borrow only what you need.
- Know your interest rate.
- Understand the total cost.
- Make a plan to repay.
- Stay disciplined and consistent.

The Power of Patience

Waiting and saving can protect your money and your future.

- Save first.
- Avoid impulse buys.
- Let your money grow.
- Build wealth over time.

Interest in Action

See how interest grows the longer you wait to repay.

Think Ahead

Every financial decision you make today affects your tomorrow.

- Think before you borrow.
- Plan before you spend.
- Choose freedom over debt.
- Your future self will thank you!

Discipline today creates options tomorrow.
Choose wisely, live freely.

Borrow today with a plan, so your future stays in your hands.

Lola's Wisdom: Borrow Carefully

Credit can help build credit history, support major needs, and create opportunity. But it can also create debt, interest, delayed freedom, and stress. Borrowing carefully today protects your peace of mind and keeps your future on track.

Key Lesson

Financial maturity requires understanding consequences.

Borrowing Can Help

- Build credit history
- Cover important needs
- Invest in education
- Start a business
- Create future opportunities

Borrowing Can Hurt

- High interest adds up
- Missed payments hurt your credit
- Debt causes stress
- Limits future choices
- Takes longer to reach your goals

Questions to Think About

1. Do I really need to borrow, or is there another option?
2. Can I afford the payments now and later?
3. Do I understand the total cost of borrowing?
4. What will happen if I miss a payment?
5. How will this loan help me reach my goals?

Before You Borrow, Do This!

- Check your budget.
- Look at your savings.
- Compare different options.
- Estimate total costs.
- Make a repayment plan.
- Talk to a trusted adult or mentor.
- Only borrow if it supports your goals.

Real-World Connection

Borrowing is a big responsibility used by adults every day—whether it's for a home, a car, or education. Smart borrowing decisions today build the confidence and freedom you'll need for a stronger future.

Smart borrowing today, brighter possibilities tomorrow.

Wise words today build financial success tomorrow.

Vocabulary Builder

Knowing these words helps you understand how borrowing works and how to make smart money choices.

	Credit	Borrowed money that must be repaid.
	Debt	Money owed.
	Interest	Extra money charged for borrowing.
	Minimum Payment	The smallest required payment.
	Due Date	The deadline for repayment.
	Credit Score	A rating that reflects borrowing reliability.
	Bonus Tip	Understanding vocabulary strengthens financial confidence.

Why Vocabulary Matters

- Helps you understand important financial ideas.
- Builds confidence when making money decisions.
- Prepares you to talk about money like a pro.
- Supports smart planning and problem-solving.
- Leads to a stronger financial future.

Word Match Activity

Match each word on the left with the correct meaning on the right.

1 Credit	A Extra money charged for borrowing.
2 Interest	B The smallest required payment.
3 Minimum Payment	C Borrowed money that must be repaid.
4 Due Date	D Money owed.
5 Debt	E The deadline for repayment.
6 Credit Score	F A rating that reflects borrowing reliability.

Quick Tips to Remember

- Always read the terms before you borrow.
- Ask questions if you don't understand something.
- Compare options before choosing a loan or card.
- Keep track of payments and due dates.
- Build good habits now for a better tomorrow.

Real-Life Scenario

Maria wants to buy a new laptop for school. She can't pay for it all today, so she takes out a loan. She reads the terms, understands the interest rate, and checks the minimum payment and due date. She makes her payments on time and keeps her credit score strong. By borrowing carefully, Maria stays stress-free and reaches her goal!

The right words today create better choices tomorrow.

Good things come to those who plan, not to those who rush. ♡

Borrow or Wait?

Smart money decisions today lead to freedom tomorrow.
Think carefully. Plan wisely. Your future self will thank you!

Instructions

For each situation, decide:
save first, borrow, responsibly, or avoid purchase.

Situation	Save First	Borrow Responsibly	Avoid Purchase
1 Gaming system you want immediately			
2 Laptop needed for school			
3 Designer clothing			

When It's Okay to Borrow

- For needs that support your education or future.
- When you have a plan to repay on time.
- When the long-term benefits are greater than the cost.
- When borrowing is part of a smart financial plan.

When It's Better to Wait or Save

- For wants that don't improve your future.
- When the cost is more than you can afford.
- When it will take too long to pay back.
- When patience can save you money.

Smart Decision Planner

Pick something you want. Decide your best move and create a plan.

What I want: ______________________________

Why I want it: ______________________________

My best move (circle one): Save First / Borrow Responsibly / Avoid Purchase

My plan: ______________________________

____

How long will it take? ____________________

How much will I need? ____________________

Date I can reach my goal: ____________________

Plan your money, protect your future, and watch your dreams come true!

Plan today.
Protect tomorrow.
Build the future
you deserve.

My Future Credit Rules

Good credit starts with smart choices and strong habits.
Your rules today shape your freedom tomorrow.

Instructions

Create personal borrowing rules that you will follow to build good credit and a strong future.

1. ______________________________
   ____
   ____
2. ______________________________
   ____
3. ______________________________
   ____
   ____
4. ______________________________
   ____
   ____

Smart Borrowing Reminders

- Borrow only when it's necessary.
- Understand all terms before you agree.
- Make every payment on time.
- Keep your debt low and manageable.
- Check your credit report and score.
- Ask for help if you need it.

Why Personal Rules Matter

- They help you make better money decisions.
- They protect you from unnecessary debt.
- They build discipline and financial confidence.
- They support your goals and dreams.
- They create a stronger, more secure future.

Reflection Questions

1. How do personal rules create stronger futures?

____
____
____

2. What could happen if you borrow without rules?

____
____
____

Bonus Challenge

Share one of your rules with a friend or family member. Explain why it's important and how it will help your future.

Write More

Write a short paragraph about how your rules will help you reach your biggest goals.

Your rules today, your freedom tomorrow.

Think before you borrow.
Plan before you spend.
Win your future!

Money Math Practice

Math helps you understand the true cost of borrowing and make smart financial decisions.

Instructions

You borrow $200.
Interest adds $20.

The Problem

You borrow $200.
Interest adds $20.

---

1. How much do you owe total?

$200 + $20 = ________________

---

2. If you pay $55 monthly,
how many months will repayment take?

Total Owed ÷ Monthly Payment = Months

________ ÷ $55 = ________ months

---

3. How much extra did borrowing cost?

Interest = ________________

Understanding the Math

- The total you owe includes the original amount plus interest.
- Your monthly payment helps you pay it back over time.
- Interest is the extra cost of borrowing.
- Knowing the math helps you plan and avoid surprises.

Bonus Challenge

Imagine you waited and saved $20 each month instead of borrowing.

- How many months would it take to save $200?

$200 ÷ $20 = ________ months

- How much would it cost you in interest by borrowing?

Answer: $________________

Good to Know

- **Interest Rate:** The percent charged when you borrow money.
- **Monthly Payment:** The amount you pay each month.
- **Borrow Wisely:** Only borrow what you truly need.
- **Pay More When You Can:** Extra payments reduce interest.
- **Check Terms:** Understand fees, due dates, and rules.
- **Plan Ahead:** Good planning today leads to freedom tomorrow.

Do the math, know the facts,
make smart money moves that last.

Tiny choices today, big consequences tomorrow.

Why Can Debt Grow Quickly?

Small borrowing decisions today can lead to big problems tomorrow.

Credit	Borrowed money that must be repaid.
Debt	Money owed.
Interest	Extra money charged for borrowing.
Minimum Payment	The smallest required payment.
Due Date	The deadline for repayment.
Credit Score	A rating that reflects borrowing reliability.
Bonus Tip	Understanding vocabulary strengthens financial confidence.

Why This Matters

- Debt can grow faster than you expect.
- Interest makes you pay more over time.
- High balances can limit your choices.
- Missing payments can hurt your credit.
- Planning helps you protect your future.

How Debt Can Grow (Example)

You borrow $200 with $20 in interest.

- You owe $220.
- You only pay the minimum.
- Interest adds up.
- It takes longer and costs more to pay off.

Smart Ways to Stay in Control

- Borrow only what you truly need.
- Pay more than the minimum whenever you can.
- Pay on time, every time.
- Keep track of your balance.
- Ask for help if you're struggling.

Real-Life Scenario

Maya wanted concert tickets and used a buy now, pay later plan. At first, it felt easy. But she missed a payment and was charged a late fee. Then another. Soon, she owed more than she expected. Maya made a plan, paid it off, and learned to save for the things she wants!

Reflection Questions

1. Why does borrowing feel harmless at first?

____

2. How can debt become overwhelming?

____

3. How does planning protect freedom?

____

The Debt Warning Signs

- Only paying the minimum each month
- Using credit for everyday expenses
- Missing or late payments
- Maxing out credit cards
- Feeling stressed about money

Debt may feel small today,
but it can steal your future tomorrow.
Plan ahead. Stay in control. Live debt-free and live free!

Plan today.
Borrow wisely.
Build your future
with confidence!

Future CEO Challenge: Smart Borrowing Scenario

Instructions

You need a computer for school but cannot afford it immediately. Make a smart plan to get it without hurting your future finances.

Reflection Questions

1. What are your options? ______________________
2. Which option costs the least long term? ______________________
3. How could budgeting help? ______________________
4. How could earning income help? ______________________

Your Options

1. Borrow from a parent or family member.
2. Get a small loan from a bank or credit union.
3. Use a "Buy Now, Pay Later" plan.
4. Save money and buy it later.
5. Earn money to buy it yourself.

Plan Your Budget

Estimate the total cost of the computer: $________

List your money sources and expenses.

Money Sources	Estimated Amount
Allowance	$________
Gift / Help from family	$________
Earnings (jobs, chores, etc.)	$________
Other	$________
Total Money Available	$________

How much more do you need? $________

Think It Through

List the pros and cons of each option you are considering.

Option: ________________

Pros:

- ________________
- ________________
- ________________

Cons:

- ________________
- ________________
- ________________

Smart Borrowing Reminders

- Borrow only what you truly need.
- Know how much it will cost in total.
- Understand the terms and due dates.
- Make payments on time.
- Avoid extra fees and late charges.
- Have a plan to pay it back.

How Could Earning Income Help?

- It gives you the money you need without borrowing.
- It builds responsibility and confidence.
- It helps you avoid interest and extra fees.
- It teaches valuable work and money skills.
- It creates more freedom for your goals.

Lolo's Advice

"Good leaders think ahead, plan carefully, and make smart money decisions."

Credit cards are tools, not free money,
Use them wisely, pay on time, and they can build your credit.
Use them carelessly, and debt can follow you.

Save today, use credit wisely, and build a strong financial future one step at a time!

Chapter Recap: Credit and Borrowing

In this chapter, Maya and Mateo learned important real-world money lessons.

- Credit is borrowed money.
- Debt grows through interest.
- Patience protects finances.
- Borrowing should be strategic.
- Discipline prevents costly mistakes.
- Financial maturity requires planning.
- Knowledge strengthens independence.

Lolo's Reminder

"Debt can be a tool if used wisely. But without discipline, it can become a heavy burden."

Key Takeaways

- Borrow only when necessary.
- Understand the full cost.
- Make payments on time.
- Avoid unnecessary debt.
- Plan for your future goals.

Good planning today leads to freedom tomorrow!

Lola's Advice

- Use credit responsibly.
- Track your spending.
- Stay within your means.
- Save for emergencies.
- Build good habits early.

Final Chapter Message

Borrowing can create opportunity. But understanding and discipline protect true financial freedom. Make smart choices today for a better tomorrow!

Credit cards give you purchasing power today.
Use them wisely, pay on time, and they can help you build credit.
Use them carelessly, and debt can hold you back.

We can enjoy life today and still spend responsibly!

Story

Maya, Mateo, Lola, and Lolo decided to enjoy a day at the park together. They brought snacks, played games, and talked about money and the choices that help build a better future.

Lesson Focus

Understanding how needs, wants, choices, and goals work together.

Big Idea

Smart money choices today create freedom and opportunities tomorrow.

The Money Cycle

Smart Choices Lead to:

- Less stress about money
- More savings and security
- More choices in the future
- Better opportunities
- A life you enjoy and feel proud of!

Did You Know?

- People who start saving in middle school are more likely to reach their goals as adults.
- Planning ahead reduces stress and helps you think more clearly.
- Discipline with money today leads to freedom tomorrow.

Every Day Choices Matter

- Pack a lunch instead of buying one.
- Compare prices before you buy.
- Save part of any money you get.
- Choose experiences over things.
- Think about long-term goals.

Small choices today lead to big results tomorrow!

"Enjoy life today, but choose wisely. What you do now shapes the life you'll love tomorrow."

We can enjoy life today and still spend responsibly!

Chapter 8

Bills and Real-Life Expenses

Understanding the true cost of adulthood before you get there.

Growing up costs money. True financial maturity includes understanding essential living expenses and planning ahead.

- Housing
- Utilities
- Groceries
- Transportation
- Internet
- Emergency savings
- Monthly obligations

Helpful Tips

- Know your needs vs. wants.
- Track your spending regularly.
- Save for emergencies first.
- Set financial goals and stick to them.
- Make smart choices today for a better tomorrow.

Essential Expenses

These are the costs most adults deal with every month.

- Rent / Mortgage
- Electricity, Water, Gas
- Groceries & Household
- Transportation (Gas, Insurance, Repairs)
- Internet & Phone
- Emergency Savings
- Subscriptions & Loans

Small choices today lead to big results tomorrow!

Chapter Goal

This chapter helps students understand the cost of everyday living and builds the habits needed to manage money wisely, live responsibly, and prepare for a stable future.

“Enjoy life today, but choose wisely.
What you do now shapes the life you'll love tomorrow.”

Understanding today prepares you for a stronger, more confident tomorrow!

Story

Real Life is Real Bills

Lola spread bills across the kitchen table. Maya looked shocked. "People pay for all of this every month?" Lola nodded. "Welcome to real life." Real life requires consistent planning.

Lesson Embedded

Financial maturity includes understanding real-world obligations.

What Are Monthly Obligations?

These are necessary expenses that must be paid regularly to live and function in the real world.

- Housing – Rent or mortgage
- Utilities – Electricity, water, gas
- Groceries – Food and household items
- Transportation – Gas, insurance, repairs
- Internet & Phone – Communication
- Emergency Savings – For unexpected costs
- Other Obligations – Subscriptions, loans, medical bills, and more

Why It Matters

- Life doesn't stop when bills come.
- Planning ahead reduces stress.
- Smart budgeting helps you reach your goals.
- Financial maturity builds freedom and choices.

Smart Habits to Build

- Track your income and expenses.
- Pay bills on time.
- Avoid unnecessary debt.
- Save a portion of what you earn.
- Review and adjust your budget regularly.

Pause and Think

- Which bills are needs?
- Which are wants?
- What happens if bills don't get paid?
- How can planning today protect your future?

Cool Activity!

Bill Sort Challenge

Look at the list below and sort each item into Needs or Wants.

- Rent
- Movie Tickets
- Internet
- Video Games
- New Sneakers
- Groceries
- Eating Out
- Water Bill
- Electricity
- Phone Plan
- Car Payment
- Netflix Subscription

After sorting, choose 3 needs and 2 wants. Write one way you can reduce a want to help cover your needs.

Real Talk

It's normal to feel overwhelmed at first. But every adult started right where you are. The key is learning now, so you can live better later!

Plan smart, live smart, everything will follow.

Choose needs first today, so you can enjoy wants tomorrow!

Story
Needs Come First

Mateo studied the bills carefully. "So before fun spending, people pay for needs first?" "Exactly," Lola said. Money was not only about buying things. It was also about stability.

Main Lesson
Needs must come before wants.

What Are Needs?

Needs are the things you must have to live, stay safe, and function.

- Housing – Rent or mortgage
- Utilities – Electricity, water, gas
- Groceries – Food and household items
- Transportation – Gas, insurance, repairs
- Internet & Phone – Communication
- Healthcare
- Insurance
- Emergency Savings

What Are Wants?

Wants are the things you would like to have but don't need to survive.

- New clothes
- The latest gadgets
- Eating out
- Entertainment & games
- Vacations
- Brand-name items
- Impulse purchases

Why Needs Come First

- They keep you safe and healthy.
- They help you avoid debt.
- They build a stable foundation.
- They give you peace of mind.
- They allow room for wants later—without guilt!

Cool Activity!
Sort It Out!

Look at the list below. Write each item in the correct column.

Rent	Groceries	Car Payment
Concert Tickets	Video Games	Fast Food
Electricity	Phone Bill	Internet
Designer Shoes	Vacation	New Tablet

Needs	Wants
____________	____________
____________	____________
____________	____________

Think About It

- What would happen if you only paid for wants?
- How do needs help you reach your goals?
- How can you delay wants without feeling left out?
- What's one want you could wait on to save money?

Smart Reminder

A good rule to remember:
"Pay for your needs today, so your wants are possible tomorrow."

Quick Tip

Use the 50/30/20 Rule:

- 50% for Needs
- 30% for Wants
- 20% for Savings & Debt Repayment

Plan smart, live smart, everything will follow.

Smart planning today leads to peace of mind tomorrow!

Story

Plan Today, Secure Tomorrow

Lola explained that many people struggle not because they never earn money, but because they never learn to prioritize wisely. Income, spending, planning, and emergency preparation all matter.

Why Planning Matters

- It helps you live within your means.
- It prepares you for unexpected situations.
- It reduces stress and worry.
- It helps you reach your goals faster.
- It builds a strong financial future.

The 4 Pillars of Financial Success

1. Income – Earn consistently.
2. Spending – Spend wisely.
3. Planning – Set goals and create a plan.
4. Preparation – Save and be ready for anything.

Helpful Habits

- Make a budget and stick to it.
- Track your spending.
- Save before you spend.
- Build an emergency fund.
- Review your goals regularly.
- Keep learning about money.

Cool Activity!

My Future Security Plan

Fill in the blanks to create your plan for a more secure future.

- My short-term goal (within 1 year): ____
- My long-term goal (5+ years): ____
- I will save this amount each month: $ ____
- My emergency plan: ____
- I will review my plan every: ____

Think Ahead!

Imagine an unexpected event happens (like a car repair or medical bill).
How would your plan help you handle it without stress?

- ____
- ____
- ____

Success today = Peace of mind tomorrow!

Money is a tool, not the goal. Smart budgeting today gives you choices now, security in the future, and freedom to live life on your terms.

Smart money choices today create a stable and stress-free future!

Lola's Wisdom:

Real Life Costs More Than Trends

Responsible financial priorities include housing, food, transportation, emergency savings, utilities, healthcare, and education.

Key Lesson

Needs create security. Wants should follow discipline.

Essential Needs vs. Wants

Needs (Must-Haves)	Wants (Nice-to-Haves)
A safe place to live	The newest gadgets
Nutritious food	Designer clothes
Reliable transportation	Eating out often
Utilities (electricity, water, gas)	Streaming subscriptions
Healthcare	Fancy cars
Education	Vacations
Emergency savings	Impulse purchases

Why Needs Come First

- They keep you safe and healthy.
- They help you avoid debt and financial stress.
- They build a strong foundation for your dreams.
- They prepare you for unexpected situations.

Financial Priorities

1. Housing
2. Food
3. Transportation
4. Utilities
5. Healthcare
6. Education
7. Emergency Savings

Then... Wants!

Lola's Life Tip

Trends fade. Needs remain. Focus on what matters most and watch your future grow!

Cool Activity!

Needs or Wants?

Decide if each item is a need or a want.
Write N for Need and W for Want.

____ Groceries	____ Phone Upgrade
____ Concert Tickets	____ Doctor Visit
____ Electricity Bill	____ Vacation
____ New Sneakers	____ Internet Bill
____ Rent / Mortgage	____ Fancy Coffee Daily

Emergency Fund Goal

Experts recommend saving 3–6 months of essential expenses.

Start small, stay consistent, and build your safety net!

Quick Reminder

Spend less on wants, so you can stress less about needs.

Cover your needs. Control your wants. Create your freedom.

Vocabulary Builder

Learning key money words helps you understand how to manage your finances and make smart choices.

Rent	Money paid for housing.
Utilities	Monthly services like electricity, water, or internet.
Groceries	Essential food purchases.
Transportation	Costs related to travel.
Emergency Fund	Savings reserved for unexpected expenses.
Monthly Expenses	Regular financial obligations.

Cool Fact!

People who track their expenses are 2x more likely to reach their financial goals!

Think It!

If you had an extra $50 this month, would you spend it on a want or add it to your emergency fund?

Did You Know?

- The average person spends over $2,000 a year on impulse buys.
- People who budget save an average of $5,000 more each year.
- Starting an emergency fund (even with $10) can keep a small problem from becoming a big one.

Real Life Example

Maya wanted new sneakers for $80. She saved $20 and waited. Two weeks later, she still wanted them but used a discount and only spent $60. She saved $20 and added it to her emergency fund!

Money Mindset

It's not about how much money you make. It's about how well you manage what you have.

Know the words. Make the plan. Create the life you want.

Household Budget Builder

Instructions

Imagine you earn $2,500 monthly.
Divide your money responsibly.

Rent	$ ________	______ %
Groceries	$ ________	______ %
Utilities	$ ________	______ %
Transportation	$ ________	______ %
Savings	$ ________	______ %
Emergency Fund	$ ________	______ %
Entertainment	$ ________	______ %
TOTAL	**$2,500**	**100%**

Budgeting Tips

- Cover your needs first.
- Save for the future.
- Plan for unexpected costs.
- Make room for things you enjoy.
- Review and adjust your budget as needed.

The 50/30/20 Rule

A simple guide to balance your budget:

50% for Needs (essentials)
30% for Wants (lifestyle)
20% for Savings & Debt Repayment

Use this rule as a starting point, then adjust to fit your life!

Reflection Questions

- Did your budget cover essentials first?
- Was your budget balanced?
- Are you saving for your future?
- What would you change about your budget?
- Do you have a plan for emergencies?

Plan today. Budget wisely. Build the future you want.

Spending Smart Challenge

Instructions

You have $100 to spend this week.
Decide where your money goes.
Make smart choices!

Groceries	$ ________	% ________
Transportation	$ ________	% ________
Utilities	$ ________	% ________
Entertainment	$ ________	% ________
Eating Out	$ ________	% ________
Education	$ ________	% ________
Savings	$ ________	% ________
Emergency Fund	$ ________	% ________
TOTAL	**$100**	**100%**

Smart Spending Tips

- Spend on what you need first.
- Save a little, even if it's small.
- Avoid impulse purchases.
- Compare prices before you buy.
- Plan ahead to avoid surprises.

Think About It!

If something you want is not in your budget, what could you do?
Write your ideas below.

____

____

____

Reflection Questions

- Did you spend more on needs or wants?
- Did you save any money?
- What was the hardest choice to make?
- What could you do differently next time?
- How can budgeting help you reach your goals?

Make a plan. Spend wisely. Save for tomorrow.

Saving for the Future

Instructions

You saved $50 this month.
Choose a savings goal and plan how to reach it.
Every dollar you save today helps your future!

Choose Your Goal:

New Bike	$ ________
New Laptop	$ ________
Family Vacation	$ ________
College Fund	$ ________
First Car	$ ________
New Home	$ ________

TOTAL GOAL $ ________

Saving Tips

- Set a goal and stay focused.
- Save a little each month.
- Avoid unnecessary spending.
- Use a savings jar or bank.
- Watch your goal grow!

Plan Your Savings

How much will you save each week?
$ ________

How long will it take to reach your goal? ________ weeks

What can you do to stay on track?

____

____

____

Reflection Questions

- Why is it important to save money?
- Which goal means the most to you?
- What can you give up to save more?
- How will reaching your goal improve your future?

Save today. Plan ahead. Build tomorrow.

Prepare today with good habits, so you can live life tomorrow with confidence!

Preparing for Real Life

Instructions

Reflect on real-life expenses.

Real-Life Expenses You May Face

- **Housing** – Rent or mortgage, property insurance, maintenance
- **Utilities** – Electricity, water, gas, internet, trash
- **Food** – Groceries, dining out, and meal planning
- **Transportation** – Car payment, gas, insurance, repairs, public transit
- **Healthcare** – Insurance, doctor visits, prescriptions
- **Education** – Tuition, books, supplies, student loans
- **Debt Payments** – Credit cards, personal loans, student loans
- **Savings & Emergency Fund** – Financial safety for the unexpected
- **Personal & Miscellaneous** – Clothing, personal care, gifts, hobbies

Why It Matters

- Life comes with planned and unplanned expenses.
- Budgeting helps you make smart choices.
- Planning today builds freedom tomorrow.
- Good habits now lead to less stress later.
- Preparation gives you confidence to handle anything.

Reflection Questions

1. What surprised me most about adulthood expenses?
____
____
2. Why is budgeting more important now?
____
____
3. What habits should I improve?
____
____
4. How can I prepare for unexpected expenses?
____
____

Helpful Tips for Real Life

- Track your spending and compare it to your needs.
- Create a monthly budget and stick to it.
- Always save a portion of your income.
- Avoid impulse purchases.
- Build an emergency fund before spending on wants.
- Pay bills on time and avoid late fees.
- Use needs versus wants to guide your decisions.
- Look for discounts, coupons, and smart deals.
- Set short-term and long-term financial goals.
- Continue learning about money and investing.

Essential Expenses

These are the costs most adults deal with every month.

- Rent / Mortgage
- Electricity, Water, Gas
- Groceries & Household
- Transportation (Gas, Insurance, Repairs)
- Internet & Phone
- Emergency Savings
- Subscriptions & Loans

Cool Activity!

Create Your Monthly Budget

1. Write down all the essential expenses from the list.
2. Estimate how much each might cost in a month.
3. Add a savings goal (at least 10% of your income).
4. Compare your total to your income.
5. Adjust your wants to stay within your budget.

My Budget Plan

Income: $ ________

Expenses:
-
-
-

Savings Goal: $ ________

Leftover: $ ________

Did You Know?

Even small expenses add up! A $5 daily coffee adds up to $1,825 in a year. Be aware. Be smart.

The habits you build **today** your the life you want tomorrow.
Be ready. Be smart. Be unstoppable.

Every conversation is a chance to learn something that can guide your future!

Money Mission: Interview an Adult

Instructions

Ask a trusted adult about real-life expenses.

Interview Questions

1. What bills surprised you most?

   ____
   ____
   ____

2. What lesson do you wish you learned earlier?

   ____
   ____
   ____

3. What advice would you give your younger self?

   ____
   ____
   ____

Reflection Question

- What did I learn from the interview?

____
____
____
____

Bonus Challenge

Wisdom often grows through listening.

Write one powerful quote or tip you heard that you will always remember.

____

Tips for a Great Interview

- Choose someone you trust.
- Be respectful and listen carefully.
- Ask follow-up questions.
- Take notes while they talk.
- Say thank you for their time and wisdom.

Cool Activity!

Expense Detective

Work with your adult to list 5 everyday expenses and 5 savings goals. Then draw a line connecting each expense to a savings goal it can support!

5 Everyday Expenses	5 Savings Goals
1. ________	1. ________
2. ________	2. ________
3. ________	3. ________
4. ________	4. ________
5. ________	5. ________

What You Can Learn

- Real-life decisions take planning.
- Money choices today affect your tomorrow.
- Listening to others helps you grow smarter.

Think About It

What is one money habit from your interview that you want to start using?

____
____
____

The more you learn today, the better choices you can make tomorrow!

Plan today.
Protect tomorrow.
Live free
every day!

Chapter 8 Recap:
Bills and Real-Life Expenses

In this chapter, Maya and Mateo learned important real-world money lessons.

- Adulthood involves major expenses
- Needs must come first
- Budgeting protects stability
- Emergency planning matters
- Prioritization creates security
- Financial maturity builds independence
- Preparation strengthens freedom

Key Takeaways

- Understand the difference between needs and wants.
- Create and follow a budget.
- Build an emergency fund.
- Use money wisely and avoid debt.
- Make smart choices for a better future.

What Did You Learn?

Write your favorite lesson from this chapter and why it is important.

____

____

____

____

Apply It to Real Life

Circle or check the action you will take this week.

- I will create or update my budget.
- I will save money for an emergency.
- I will spend less on wants and more on needs.
- I will track my spending.
- I will talk to a trusted adult about money goals.
- I will make a plan for my future.

Reflection Time

Answer the questions below.

1. What was the most important thing you learned in this chapter?

   ____

   ____

2. How will you use what you learned in real life?

   ____

   ____

3. What is one money goal you have for your future?

   ____

Final Chapter Message

Financial success is not only about earning.
It is about protecting, prioritizing, and planning for real life.

Big dreams start with smart choices today!

Chapter 9
Investing and Growing Money

Learning how money can work for you over time.

Saving protects money. Investing can help money grow. This chapter introduces early wealth-building principles in age-appropriate ways.

- Investing basics
- Assets
- Risk
- Growth
- Compound progress
- Wealth-building habits

Did You Know?

The earlier you start investing, the more time your money has to grow!

Design Goal

Coins growing into a tree beside Maya and Mateo's future goals board with savings jars, growth charts, and investment icons.

What You'll Learn

- What it means to invest
- What assets are
- Why risk is part of investing
- How growth happens over time
- The power of compound progress
- Habits that build long-term wealth

Why It Matters

- Helps money work for you
- Creates more opportunities
- Builds a stronger future
- Teaches smart decision-making
- Encourages patience and discipline
- Opens the door to financial freedom

Tips from Lolo

- Start early and stay consistent.
- Learn something new every day.
- Don't be afraid to ask questions.
- Make smart choices with your money.
- Focus on the long term, not quick wins.
- Surround yourself with positive influences.

Cool Activity: My Wealth Tree

Draw a tree. Write or draw things you want to achieve in the leaves. Write the habits or smart choices that will help your money grow in the roots.

My Goals (Leaves):	My Smart Habits (Roots):
1. ______	1. ______
2. ______	2. ______
3. ______	3. ______
4. ______	4. ______

Reflection Questions

1. What is one thing you learned about investing today?
______
______
2. Why is it important to be patient when investing?
______
______
3. How can smart habits help your money grow over time?
______

Save today.
Invest wisely.
Build security.
Create opportunities.
Secure your future!

Story

Lolo placed two jars on the table. "One jar protects money," he explained. "The other helps money grow." Maya asked how money could grow. "When used wisely, money can work for you," Lolo said.

Lesson Embedded

Saving protects.
Investing grows.

Key Takeaway

- Saving keeps your money safe for today.
- Investing helps your money grow for tomorrow.
- Both saving and investing are important.
- Smart choices now create a better future.

Saving vs. Investing

Saving	Investing
Keeps money safe	Helps money grow
Easy to access	May have more risk
Lower returns	Higher potential returns
Short-term goals	Long-term goals

Examples

Saving Example:
You save $20 a week for a new backpack.

Investing Example:
You invest $20 each week so your money can grow for your future.

Cool Activity: Sort It Out!

Decide if each item is something you should SAVE for or INVEST in. Write "S" in the circle if it's for Saving. Write "I" if it's for Investing.

New Bicycle ○	Travel Fund ○	New Camera ○
New Phone ○	Emergency Fund ○	Video Game ○
College Education ○	Stocks or Funds ○	Start a Business ○

Reflection Questions

1. Why is it important to save before you invest?
____
____

2. What are some things you would like to invest in one day?
____
____

3. How can investing help you reach your future goals?
____
____

Invest today, build tomorrow, and create a future full of possibilities!

Save today.
Invest wisely.
Build security.
Create opportunities.
Secure your future!

Story

Lolo explained that investing means using money strategically to build future opportunities. Growth often happens slowly. Maya learned that wealth is rarely instant.

"The other helps money grow." Maya asked how money could grow.

"When used wisely, money can work for you," Lolo said.

Main Lesson

Patience often builds greater financial strength.

Key Takeaway

Investing is a long-term plan. Small steps today, big results tomorrow.

Why It Matters

- Growth takes time, but it is worth it.
- Patience helps your money grow stronger.
- Long-term thinking leads to bigger opportunities.
- Smart investors focus on progress, not speed.
- Time is one of the most powerful tools in investing.
- Steady steps beat fast wins in the long run.

Saving vs. Investing

Saving	Investing
Keeps money safe	Helps money grow
Easy to access	May have more risk
Lower returns	Higher potential returns
Short-term goals	Long-term goals

Tips from Lolo

- Start early, even if it's a small amount.
- Be patient and let your money grow.
- Don't rush—good things take time.
- Keep learning and stay consistent.
- Focus on the future, not just today.
- Trust the process and stay the course.

Cool Activity: Growth Timeline

Imagine you invest $10 today and it grows over time. Fill in the timeline below with how much it could grow with a small annual return.

Year 1	Year 5	Year 10	Year 20	Year 30
$______	$______	$______	$______	$______

What did you learn?

____

____

Reflection Questions

1. What did Lolo explain about investing?

____

2. Why is patience important when investing?

____

3. How can slow growth lead to big opportunities?

____

4. What will you do today to plan for your future?

____

Good things take time, great things take patience!

Story

Mateo understood that long-term habits could create stronger futures than short-term spending. Maya began seeing money not as something to spend quickly, but as something that could build dreams.

Key Takeaway

Wealth-building is a long-term process.

What You Should Remember

Good habits today create strong financial foundations for tomorrow.

Why It Matters

- Long-term habits help you reach your biggest goals.
- Small choices each day lead to big results over time.
- Delaying instant rewards can build future freedom.
- Financial discipline builds confidence and security.
- Your future self benefits from today's good choices.
- Dreams grow when you plan for the future.

Tips from Lolo

- Think about what you want in the future.
- Save and invest consistently.
- Avoid unnecessary spending.
- Be patient—success takes time.
- Stay focused on your goals.
- Celebrate progress, not just results.

Cool Activity: Future You Letter

Write a letter to your future self 10 years from now. Describe your goals, the habits you will keep, and the kind of life you want to build.

Dear Future Me,

____

____

____

From,

____

Lolo's Tip

Your future is built by the habits you choose today. Stay consistent, stay focused, and your future self will be proud of you!

Why understanding long habits makes a big difference in one's future.

Lolo's Legacy Lesson: Think Long Term

Saving is powerful, but strategic growth even greater possibilities. Investing can build wealth, strengthens security, support larger goals, create opportunity, and teach discipline.

What This Means

Build Wealth
Investing helps your money grow over time and creates financial freedom.

Strengthen Security
Smart money choices protect you and your loved ones.

Support Goals
Long-term planning helps you reach big dreams like a home, education, or travel.

Create Opportunity
Growth opens doors to new experiences and greater possibilities.

Teach Discipline
Investing teaches patience, focus, and self-control.

Why Long-Term Thinking Matters

- Small steps today can lead to big results tomorrow.
- Time is your greatest advantage when investing.
- Consistency builds momentum and confidence.
- Wealth is built slowly, but it lasts longer.
- Financial freedom comes from smart habits over time.

Tips for Long-Term Success

- Start early, even if it's a small amount.
- Save and invest regularly.
- Stay patient—let your money grow.
- Make smart choices and avoid debt.
- Keep learning about money and investing.
- Review your goals and stay on track.

Cool Activity: Future Freedom Plan

Fill in the steps you will take to create more freedom in your life.

1. One goal I want to achieve: ____________________
2. One habit I will build: ____________________
3. One thing I will save for: ____________________
4. One way I will invest in my future: ____________
5. One thing I will do to keep learning: ____________

Reflection Questions

1. What is the main idea of this lesson? ____________________
2. Why is long-term growth better than short-term spending? ____________________
3. How can investing help you in the future? ____________________
4. What is one smart financial habit you can start today? ____________________

Great things take time, but the results are worth it!

Vocabulary Builder

Learning important money words helps you understand how to build wealth and make smart financial decisions. Use these words in your daily life!

Invest	To use money in ways that may help it grow. *Example: I invest my money to build a better future.*
Asset	Something valuable that can build wealth. *Example: A house, business, or savings account is an asset.*
Risk	The possibility of loss. *Example: All investments have some level of risk.*
Return	Growth or profit earned. *Example: My investment gave me a good return.*
Compound Growth	Money growing over time through consistency. *Example: Interest earns more interest over time.*
Long-Term Goal	A future objective that requires patience and planning. *Example: Buying a house is a long-term goal.*

Cool Activity: Match It!

Match each vocabulary word with its correct meaning.

1 Invest •	A Growth or profit earned.
2 Asset •	B Something valuable that can build wealth.
3 Risk •	C The possibility of loss.
4 Return •	D To use money in ways that may help it grow.
5 Compound Growth •	E Money growing over time through consistency.
6 Long-Term Goal •	F A future objective that requires patience and planning.

Think & Write

Choose three vocabulary words above and write one sentence for each.

1. ______________________________
2. ______________________________
3. ______________________________

Words build knowledge, and knowledge builds your future!

My Money Growth Tracker

Instructions

Imagine you save $20 monthly. Track your progress.

- After 6 Months $_______________
- After 12 Months $_______________
- After 24 Months $_______________

Did You Know?

Small amounts saved consistently can grow into big opportunities over time!

My Savings Growth Table

Time	Monthly Savings	Total Saved	What I Could Do With It
6 Months	$20	$______	________
12 Months	$20	$______	________
24 Months	$20	$______	________

Remember: Consistency today creates freedom tomorrow.

Reflection Questions

1. How does consistency build larger results?

____

____

____

2. What goals could this savings support?

____

____

____

Bonus Challenge

How would increasing your savings accelerate growth?

If I save $__________ instead of $20 monthly, here's how it could help:

____

____

____

Simple Ways to Save More

- Track your spending and find areas to cut back.
- Set a savings goal and stick to it.
- Automate your savings if possible.
- Avoid impulse purchases.
- Save any extra money you earn.

I make smart money choices today for a better tomorrow!

My Future Wealth Goals

Instructions

Set short-term and long-term financial goals.

Short-Term Goal (Within 1 Year)

My Goal: ____________________

Why It's Important: ____________________

____

How Much It May Cost: $ ____________________

Target Date: ____________________

Steps I Will Take:

1. ____________________
2. ____________________
3. ____________________

Long-Term Goal (1 Year and Beyond)

My Goal: ____________________

Why It's Important: ____________________

____

How Much It May Cost: $ ____________________

Target Date: ____________________

Steps I Will Take:

1. ____________________
2. ____________________
3. ____________________

Reflection Questions

1. What habits support these goals? ____________________

____

2. How can saving and investing strengthen them? ____________________

____

3. What sacrifices may help accelerate progress? ____________________

____

Tips for Reaching Your Goals

- Write your goals down and keep them visible.
- Break big goals into smaller, doable steps.
- Save consistently, even small amounts count.
- Invest wisely for long-term growth.
- Review and adjust your goals regularly.

Cool Activity: Dream Board

Draw or write pictures of things you're working toward. It could be a home, a car, a trip, or financial freedom!

Place your dream board somewhere you will see it every day to stay motivated.

I take control of my money today to build the future I dream of!

Money Math Practice

Instructions

You save $15 monthly.

Did You Know?

Even saving small amounts regularly can help you reach big goals over time!

My Savings Growth Table

Time Period	Monthly Savings	Total Saved	What I Could Do With It
1 Month	$15	$______	______ ______
6 Months	$15	$______	______ ______
1 Year (12 Months)	$15	$______	______ ______
3 Years (36 Months)	$15	$______	______ ______

Tip: Small amounts saved consistently can lead to big results!

Reflection Questions

1. How much will you save in one year?
   $______________________
2. How much in three years?
   $______________________
3. If you increase to $25 monthly, how much more could you build?
   ____
   ____

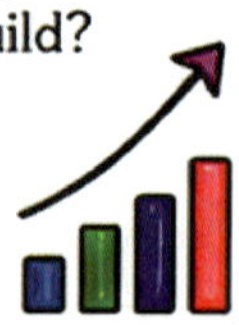

Money Math Practice

Solve each problem below.

1. If you save $15 every month, how much will you save in 2 years? (24 months)
   Answer: $__________
2. If you save $15 every month, how much will you save in 5 years? (60 months)
   Answer: $__________
3. If you save $30 every month, how much will you save in 3 years? (36 months)
   Answer: $__________
4. If you save $50 every month, how much will you save in 1 year? (12 months)
   Answer: $__________

Bonus Challenge

You receive a $100 bonus.
If you add it to your savings today, how will it impact your 3-year total?

New 3-Year Total: $______________

What could this extra money help you do?

____

____

Smart Saving Tips

- Set a goal and write it down.
- Pay yourself first—save before you spend.
- Be consistent, even when the amount is small.
- Look for ways to earn extra money.
- Track your progress and celebrate wins!

Your future is created by what you do today, not tomorrow. Keep saving, keep growing, keep going!

Good things take time, but they are worth it in the end!

Why Is Patience Powerful?

Instructions

Reflect on delayed gratification.

Reflection Questions

1. Why do many people struggle with delayed gratification?

____

____

2. How can long-term thinking strengthen my future?

____

____

3. What habits should I improve now?

____

____

What Is Delayed Gratification?

It means choosing to wait for a bigger reward instead of taking a smaller reward right away. It helps you make better choices for your future.

✗ Instant Choice

Get a small treat now.

✓ Future Choice

Wait and get something better later!

The Power of Patience

Patience helps you to:

- Reach bigger goals
- Make smarter decisions
- Build strong habits
- Earn trust and respect
- Create more opportunities

Short-Term vs. Long-Term Thinking

	Short-Term Thinking	Long-Term Thinking
Focus	What feels good right now.	What is best for my future.
Result	Small rewards, short satisfaction.	Big rewards, lasting happiness.
Example	Spending all my money on games today.	Saving and investing for my dreams.

Activity: Choose Your Future

Read each situation and circle the choice that shows patience.

1. You get $10 today or $30 in one month.
2. Study for 30 minutes now or relax and risk a bad grade.
3. Buy a cheap toy now or save for the bike you really want.
4. Post for likes now or focus on a goal that builds your future.

$10 today	or	$30 in one month
Relax now	or	Study now
Buy toy now	or	Save for bike
Post now	or	Focus on my goal

Patience today is the key to freedom tomorrow.
Stay focused, keep believing, and never give up!

The seeds you plant today will grow your future tomorrow.

Chapter 9 Recap: Investing and Growing Money

In this chapter, Maya and Mateo learned important real-world money lessons.

- Saving protects money
- Investing grows money
- Patience matters
- Discipline builds opportunity
- Long-term thinking strengthens security
- Small habits create larger outcomes
- Wealth often grows gradually

Final Chapter Message

Financial freedom is often built slowly, wisely, and intentionally.

Key Takeaways

1. Save regularly to protect your future.
2. Invest wisely to grow your money.
3. Be patient—big results take time.
4. Discipline today creates opportunity tomorrow.
5. Think long-term for greater security.
6. Small habits lead to big outcomes.

Why It Matters

- Helps you reach your goals
- Gives you more choices in life
- Builds confidence and independence
- Creates financial freedom
- Leaves a positive impact on others

Apply What You Learned

How can you use these lessons in your everyday life?

1. ______________________________
2. ______________________________
3. ______________________________

Smart Money Habits to Keep

- Set goals and write them down.
- Save a portion of what you earn.
- Learn about investing and try it wisely.
- Avoid unnecessary spending.
- Be patient and stay consistent.
- Keep improving your money skills.

Little by little, day by day, great things will come your way.
Stay focused, stay committed, and keep growing!

Your story has power. Share it, build it, and watch it change lives.

Chapter 10
Storytelling, Branding, and Self-Publishing

Turning creativity into influence, products, and future opportunities.

Creativity can become opportunity. Ideas can become books, educational products, businesses, brands, and community influence.

- Books
- Educational products
- Businesses
- Brands
- Community influence

The Power of Storytelling

Stories connect, inspire, and teach. They help others learn from your experiences and ideas.

Good stories:

- Are honest and meaningful
- Solve a problem or share a lesson
- Create an emotional connection
- Leave a lasting impact

Building Your Brand

Your brand is how people remember and trust you.

Think about:

- Your values
- Your mission
- Your unique style
- How you help others

Self-Publishing Basics

Self-publishing lets you share your work with the world.

Steps to get started:

1. Write and edit your content.
2. Design a great cover.
3. Format your book or product.
4. Choose a platform to publish.
5. Promote and share your work.

Ways to Share Your Ideas

Your work can reach more people in many ways.

- Books
- Online Courses
- Workshops & Events
- Digital Products
- Social Media & Community

Extra Ideas:

- Start a blog or YouTube channel.
- Speak at school or community events.
- Collaborate with others and grow together.

Your ideas are valuable. Your voice matters. Your future is created by what you build today.

Big ideas start small, but their impact can be huge! ♡

Story

Maya loved creativity, stories, and designing ideas.

Maya and Mateo spent the afternoon dreaming and brainstorming. They imagined books, journals, posters, and digital products that could educate, inspire, and solve real problems.

Lola joined them and shared an important reminder. “Ideas become powerful when they solve problems, help others, and are shared with purpose,” she said.

Together, they learned that creative ideas, when shared with purpose, can grow into products that inspire, educate, and change lives.

Lesson Embedded

Creative ideas can become real products.

When we share our ideas, we can inspire others and create positive change. ♡

Did You Know?

- Students who budget are more likely to reach their financial goals.
- Even small amounts saved regularly can grow over time.
- Planning now helps you handle surprises later.

Why It Matters

- Good ideas can solve real problems.
- Sharing ideas can improve lives.
- Your work can inspire others.
- Creativity can build a better future.
- You have the power to make a difference in your community. ♡

From Idea to Product

Idea → Plan → Create → Product → Impact

Every product starts with an idea. With a plan and action, it can grow into something that helps many people and makes a lasting difference.

Examples of Ideas

- Educational workbooks
- Study journals
- Small business guides
- Motivational books
- Community projects

Your ideas today can change tomorrow.
Believe in your creativity. Share it with the world!

Turn your ideas into solutions that change lives!

Story

Lolo explained that every successful product begins with solving a problem. Maya and Mateo brainstormed educational workbooks, study journals, small business guides, motivational books, and community projects.

Key Takeaway

Innovation often begins with solving meaningful needs.

Why It Matters

- Growth takes time, but it is worth it.
- Patience helps your money grow stronger.
- Long-term thinking leads to bigger opportunities.
- Smart investors focus on progress, not speed.
- Time is one of the most powerful tools in investing.
- Steady steps beat fast wins in the long run.

From Idea to Product

Idea → Plan → Create → Product → Impact

Every product starts with an idea. With a plan and action, it can grow into something that helps many people and makes a lasting difference.

Examples of Ideas

- Educational workbooks
- Study journals
- Small business guides
- Motivational books
- Community projects

Activity: My Creative Plan

Choose an idea you are excited about and fill in your plan.

1. My Idea: ______________________________
2. What problem does it solve? ______________
3. What will I create? ______________________
4. Who will it help? _______________________
5. What impact do I want to make? __________

Reflection Questions

1. Why is it important to share our ideas? __________
2. How can my idea make a difference? __________
3. Who do I want to inspire with my idea? __________
4. What is one step I can take today to bring my idea to life? __________

Build a business that solves problems, shares value, and brings you joy. Do what you love, and success will follow!

Ideas have power. You have purpose!

Story

Maya realized strong brands often begin with meaningful ideas. Her creativity was not small. It could become something powerful.

Key Takeaway

Great ideas become powerful when you take action and stay consistent.

Why It Matters

- Great ideas start with caring.
- Solving needs creates real value.
- Innovation makes life better.
- Small ideas can grow into big opportunities.
- Your creativity can change lives—and the world.

From Idea to Impact

Idea → Plan → Create → Product → Impact

When you solve a meaningful need, your idea can grow into a product, a brand, or a business that helps many people.

Examples of Meaningful Ideas

- Eco-friendly water bottles
- Budgeting apps for teens
- Healthy snack brands
- Study tools and planners
- Books that inspire and educate

Activity: Need to Idea

Choose a need you see around you and turn it into an idea.

1. What need did you choose? ____________________
2. Who has this need? ____________________
3. What idea can solve it? ____________________
4. How will it help people? ____________________
5. What would success look like? ____________________

Reflection Questions

1. What did Maya learn in this story? ____________
2. Why do meaningful ideas lead to strong brands? ____
3. How can innovation help others? ____________
4. What is one idea you have that could make a difference? ____________

Do what you love, turn it into your idea, and let your idea turn into your future!

Build value.
Earn trust.
Inspire change.

Lolo's Legacy Lesson: Build More Than a Product

Successful creators build trust, value, and purpose. Strong brands focus on helping others, solving problems, clear communication, presentation, consistency, and leadership.

Key Lesson

Great brands are built through value, trust, and purpose.

Why It Matters

- Trust keeps people coming back.
- Value makes your brand unique.
- Purpose gives your brand meaning.
- Strong brands solve real problems.
- When you help others, your brand makes a lasting impact.

The 6 Pillars of a Strong Brand

1. Helping Others – Solve real problems.
2. Clear Communication – Be honest and easy to understand.
3. Presentation – Make it appealing and professional.
4. Consistency – Stay reliable and true to your message.
5. Leadership – Lead by example and inspire others.
6. Purpose – Build with meaning and make a difference.

Think Like a Creator

- Focus on people, not just profits.
- Build relationships, not just sales.
- Share your message clearly.
- Keep improving and stay committed.
- Leave a legacy, not just a product.

Activity: Brand Builder

Choose a brand you admire and answer the questions below.

1. What problem does this brand solve? ____________
2. What value does this brand provide? ____________
3. How does this brand communicate clearly? ____________
4. What makes this brand stand out? ____________
5. What is this brand's purpose or mission? ____________

Reflection Questions

1. Why is trust important in building a brand? ____________
2. How does helping others build a strong brand? ____________
3. What can you do to communicate more clearly? ____________
4. How can you lead and inspire others through your ideas? ___
5. What kind of legacy do you want your brand to leave? ____

When you build with heart, help with purpose, and lead with kindness, your brand becomes your legacy.

Vocabulary Builder

Brand	A recognizable identity for a product, service, or creator.
Marketing	Promoting products or ideas.
Publishing	Creating and sharing written or educational materials.
Product	Something created to provide value.
Audience	The people you aim to help or serve.
Public Speaking	Communicating ideas confidently to others.

Bonus Tip
Understanding vocabulary strengthens financial confidence.

Cool Facts

- Strong brands are 3 times more likely to earn customer trust.
- Books and educational content can reach and help people all over the world.
- Clear communication is one of the top skills of successful entrepreneurs.
- When you solve problems, you create value — and value builds a legacy.
- People remember how you make them feel, not just what you sell.

Build Your Brand Mindset

- Be helpful. Look for ways to solve problems in your school, home, or community.
- Be consistent. Show up, keep learning, and keep improving.
- Be you. Your story, your voice, and your ideas are powerful.
- Be patient. Great things take time and effort.
- Be generous. Share your knowledge and encourage others.

Your ideas are valuable. Your voice matters.
Use what you learn to build something that helps others!

"A great brand turns an idea into something people remember and believe in."

My First Brand Builder

Instructions

Design your own product, service, or creative idea.

- Product Name ______________________________
- What problem does it solve? ______________________________
____
- Who does it help? ______________________________
____
- Brand Message ______________________________
____
- Logo Idea (Draw or describe your logo below)

Reflection Questions

- Why would people trust this brand? ______________________________
____
- How does this product create value? ______________________________
____
- What makes it unique? ______________________________

Bonus Challenge

Create a slogan. ______________________________
____

Think like a creator, plan like a leader, and build a brand that makes a difference!

Great stories create connection, build trust, and make your idea unforgettable!

Storytelling for Business

A strong story makes your product or brand meaningful and memorable.

People don't just remember facts — they remember how a story makes them feel. Use storytelling to inspire, explain, and connect.

Key Parts of a Great Story

1. **What inspired it**
   Share the idea or moment that started it all.
2. **Who it helps**
   Describe the people or community it is for.
3. **Why it matters**
   Explain the impact and the difference it makes.
4. **How it solves problems**
   Show how your product or idea creates a solution.

Write Your Story or Message

Use the key parts above to create a short story that explains your product, service, or idea.

____

____

____

____

____

Storytelling Tips

- Know your audience.
- Keep your message clear and simple.
- Focus on the problem and the solution.
- Use emotions to create connection.
- Show the impact your idea makes.
- End with a strong call to action.

Reflection Questions

- How does storytelling strengthen marketing?

____

- Why do people connect with stories?

____

Bonus Challenge

Think of a brand or person you admire.
What story do they tell well?

____

____

____

Your story has **POWER**. Share it with **CONFIDENCE**, **INSPIRE** others, and build something **AMAZING!**

Money Math Practice

Math helps you plan, track, and grow your money wisely!

Instructions

Maya creates journals that cost $4 each to produce.

She sells them for $12 each.

She sells 25 journals.

Reflection Questions

1. What is total revenue? ____________________
2. What is total production cost? ____________________
3. What is total profit? ____________________
4. If she reinvests $50 into branding, how much remains? ____________________

Show Your Work

1. Total revenue = Selling price × Quantity

   ----

2. Total production cost = Cost per item × Quantity

   ----

3. Total profit = Revenue − Production cost

   ----

4. Amount remaining = Profit − Branding investment

Quick Summary

Selling price per journal:	$ ________
Cost to produce per journal:	$ ________
Journals sold:	________
Total revenue:	$ ________
Total production cost:	$ ________
Total profit:	$ ________
Branding investment:	$ ________
Amount remaining:	$ ________

Think Like an Entrepreneur

1. If Maya wants to sell 50 journals, what would be her total profit before branding? ________
2. If her cost to produce each journal increases to $5, how does that change her profit for 25 journals? ________
3. What are some other ways Maya could use her profit to grow her business? ________

Use math. Make smart choices. Grow your business!

Creativity turns ideas into opportunities and dreams into reality.

How Can Creativity Build My Future?

Instructions

Reflect on talents and opportunities.

Reflection Questions

1. What creative strengths do I have? ______________________
2. How could my ideas help others? ______________________
3. Could creativity become income? ______________________

Ways Creativity Can Shape Your Future

- ☑ Solves problems in new and better ways
- ☑ Helps you stand out and share your gifts
- ☑ Opens doors to jobs and businesses
- ☑ Builds confidence and leadership
- ☑ Creates impact and helps others
- ☑ Can lead to income and independence

Creative Ideas I'm Excited About

1. ______________________
____
2. ______________________
____
3. ______________________

My Action Steps

What can I do this week to grow my creativity?

1. ______________________
2. ______________________
3. ______________________

Creative Ideas That Can Earn Income

List ways your creativity could become a business or side hustle.

1. ______________________
2. ______________________
3. ______________________

Creativity is intelligence having fun.
Use your imagination today to build the life you want tomorrow.

Your ideas have the power to solve problems and inspire others!

Future CEO Challenge: My First Product Pitch

Instructions

Create a 30-second presentation for your product, book, or business idea.

What to Include in Your Pitch

1. Product name – What is your product, book, or business idea?
2. Problem solved – What problem does it solve?
3. Audience – Who is it for?
4. Why it matters – Why is this important?
5. Why people should choose it – What makes it special?

30-Second Pitch Structure

1. Start strong – Grab attention in the first 5 seconds.
2. Explain the problem – In 5–10 seconds.
3. Share your solution – In 10–20 seconds.
4. Explain the impact – In 20–25 seconds.
5. End with a call to action – In 25–30 seconds.

Reflection Questions

1. How can I speak with confidence and clarity? ______________________

____

Tips for a Great Pitch

- Know your idea inside and out.
- Speak clearly and confidently.
- Make eye contact and smile.
- Keep it short, simple, and exciting.
- Practice, practice, practice!

Plan Your Pitch

Product name: ______________________
Problem solved: ______________________
Audience: ______________________
Why it matters: ______________________
Why people should choose it: ______________________

____

My 30-Second Pitch Script

0–5 sec: ______________________
5–10 sec: ______________________
10–20 sec: ______________________
20–25 sec: ______________________
25–30 sec: ______________________

Your ideas. Your voice. Your future.
Pitch it like a leader and watch doors open!

Your story has the power to inspire, lead, and leave a legacy.

Chapter 10 Recap: Storytelling, Branding, and Self-Publishing

In this chapter, Maya and Mateo learned important real-world money lessons.

Storytelling can become business

Your stories and ideas can solve problems and create value for others.

Branding builds trust

A strong brand helps people remember you and believe in what you do.

Publishing creates products

Turning your ideas into books, planners, or digital products helps others and earns income.

Communication strengthens leadership

Speaking and listening well helps you lead, inspire, and work with others.

Creativity can solve problems

Creative thinking helps you find new ways to solve challenges and stand out.

Public speaking expands influence

Sharing your ideas with confidence helps you connect and make an impact.

Innovation creates opportunity

New ideas and bold actions open doors to exciting possibilities.

Final Chapter Message

Your ideas have value.
When paired with strategy, creativity can build powerful futures.

"Follow your passion. Believe in your ideas. Take action. Your dreams are worth it."

The future belongs to those who prepare for it today.

Final Master Recap: Building a Future Rich Mindset

Throughout their journey, Maya and Mateo discovered that financial confidence is built one smart decision at a time.

Smart Spending Protects Goals
Make thoughtful choices and spend with purpose to reach your dreams.

Budgeting Creates Freedom
A budget helps you take control of your money and your future.

Banking Builds Structure
Banks keep your money safe and help you grow it over time.

Credit Requires Discipline
Use credit wisely, pay on time, and build a strong financial reputation.

Entrepreneurship Builds Opportunity
Spot problems, create solutions, and turn ideas into income.

Leadership Strengthens Success
Great leaders inspire others and build strong, successful teams.

Creativity Can Become Business
Your ideas and creativity can solve problems and create real value.

Investing Grows Wealth
Investing your money today can build wealth for tomorrow.

Public Speaking Expands Influence
Sharing your voice with confidence helps you lead and make an impact.

Storytelling Can Create Products
Your stories can educate, inspire, and even become products.

Final Core Lesson
True financial confidence is not about being rich overnight.

It is about building knowledge, discipline, leadership, and courage over time.

Empowerment Reminder
Every smart choice today strengthens tomorrow.

Your future grows when your passion meets purpose.
Keep creating, keep learning, and never stop believing in your ideas!

Your mindset today shapes the opportunities tomorrow.

Final Reflection Page: My Future Rich Mindset

Instructions

Reflect on your journey and write one commiitment you will begin today.

Reflection Questions

- What financial lesson changed my thinking most? ______________________
- What habits do I want to improve now? ______________________
- What are my future financial goals? ______________________
- How can I become a stronger leader? ______________________
- How can creativity strengthen my future? ______________________
- What kind of legacy do I want to build? ______________________

My Commitment

One commitment I will begin today:

____

____

____

"The best investment you can make is in yourself. Keep growing, keep going, and build the future you deserve!"

Bonus Savings Tracker: My Long-Term Savings Log

Instructions

Track your monthly savings goals and build the habit of saving consistently.
Small steps today lead to big results tomorrow!

Month

____

Savings Goal $

____

Amount Saved $

____

Remaining Goal $

____

Reflection Questions

- Am I improving consistency?

____
____

- What habits support growth?

____
____

- How can I strengthen discipline?

____
____

Bonus Challenge

Set one yearly savings goal.

____

Tip: Break your goal into monthly steps to stay on track!

WHY SAVING MATTERS

Saving gives you choices, freedom, and peace of mind.
It helps you prepare for the future and reach your dreams!

Examples of Long-Term Goals

- College Education
- Buying a Home
- Starting a Business
- Traveling the World
- Helping Others

HOW TO STAY ON TRACK

Set Clear Goals
Know what you're saving for and how much you need.

Save Regularly
Set aside a portion of your money every month.

Track Progress
Check your progress and celebrate wins!

Avoid Temptations
Spend wisely and focus on what matters most.

Stay Motivated
Keep your goals in mind and never give up!

You've Got This!

Every dollar you save is a step closer to your dreams. Be patient with yourself, stay consistent, and believe in your future.

Your future self will thank you!

Remember:

Discipline + Patience + Consistency = Success

Keep saving today for a brighter tomorrow!

"A little saving today creates a lot of freedom tomorrow."
– Unknown

Your future is created by what you do today, not tomorrow.

Vision Board Page: My Future Goals

Instructions

Create your personal future vision.

- Education goals
- Career goals
- Business goals
- Savings goals
- Travel goals
- Leadership goals
- Creative goals
- Health & Wellness goals
- Family & Relationships goals
- Personal Growth goals
- Giving Back goals

Reflection Question

- What habits today can help me build this future?

____

____

____

____

SMART Goals Guide

Make your goals SMART!

- S **Specific** – Be clear about what you want.
- M **Measurable** – Track your progress.
- A **Achievable** – Set goals you can reach.
- R **Relevant** – Make sure it matters to you.
- T **Time-bound** – Give it a deadline.

Additional Tips for Your Vision Board

- Be specific about what you want.
- Use pictures, words, and colors that inspire you.
- Think about short-term and long-term goals.
- Place your vision board where you will see it daily.
- Believe in yourself and stay focused!

"The future belongs to those who believe in the beauty of their dreams."
– Eleanor Roosevelt

The more you learn today, the more you earn tomorrow.

Vocabulary Builder

Budget	A plan for how money is used.
Savings	Money set aside for later.
Income	Money earned or received.
Expense	Money spent.
Credit	Borrowed money that must be repaid.
Debt	Money owed.
Interest	Extra money earned or charged.
Bank	A place that stores and manages money.
Profit	Money remaining after costs.
Revenue	Total money earned before expenses.
Asset	Something valuable that can build wealth.
Investing	Using money in ways that may help it grow.
Branding	Creating an identity for a product or business.
Marketing	Promoting products or ideas.
Entrepreneurship	Creating a business or solution.
Leadership	Guiding and inspiring others.

Bonus Tip

Understanding vocabulary strengthens financial confidence.

"Knowledge is the seed, action is the water, and growth is the reward." – Zig Ziglar

You are capable of amazing things. Keep learning, keep growing, and never stop believing in yourself! ♡

Final Closing Page: Keep Building Boldly

Your future is in your hands, and every choice you make today helps shape the person you will become tomorrow and beyond. Your future will not be shaped by trends alone. It will be shaped by smart decisions, financial wisdom, leadership, creativity, discipline, and courage.

Dream Big. Spend Smart. Lead Boldly. Build Your Future.

Congratulations, Future Leaders!

You did it! You have successfully completed this workbook through the workshop. We are so proud of your dedication, effort, and commitment to growing your financial knowledge and building an entrepreneurial mindset.

This book was created to:

- Teach you smart money habits and real-world skills.
- Inspire your creativity and entrepreneurial thinking.
- Guide you in setting goals and making wise decisions.
- Empower you to take charge of your future.

As you enter high school and beyond...

- Keep learning and stay curious.
- Use your knowledge and skills in everyday life.
- Stay focused, stay kind, and keep pushing forward.
- Remember: You have the power to create the future you envision.

Your journey is just beginning. Keep building boldly, keep believing in yourself, and never stop dreaming, planning, and taking action.

The best is yet to come!

Keep believing in your dreams, even when the journey feels slow. Every smart choice, brave step, and kind action is helping build the future you were meant for.
– Unknown

Certificate of Completion

Proudly Awarded To

____

This certifies that the student below has completed the

Discover Your Potential & Future

workbook.

Skills & Growth Achieved

Goal Setting | Exploring Interests | Building Confidence | Growth Mindset | Learning Strategies | Future Planning

Student Name: ______________________________

Date: ______________________________

Signature: ______________________________

The best investment you can make is in yourself.

Dear Future Leaders

Dear Reader,

Thank you for joining Maya and Mateo on this journey. We hope this workbook has shown you that your future is not built by luck alone. It is built through knowledge, discipline, courage, leadership, creativity, and smart choices.

Whether you dream of owning a business, helping your family, traveling the world, publishing books, or becoming financially independent, you are capable of building something extraordinary.

Final Encouragement

Dream wisely. Spend smart. Lead boldly. Build your future.

With encouragement,

Mona Liza Santos :)

You've Completed This Workbook!

Keep using what you've learned, keep asking questions, and keep taking action. Your future is in your hands, and **the best is yet to come!**

Keep dreaming.
Keep learning.
Keep growing.
Keep going!

You are the leader of your future. Make it amazing!

FUTURE LEADERS PLEDGE

My Promise to Myself

As I continue my journey, I promise to keep learning, growing, and believing in what I can become.

- I will believe in myself.
- I will make smart choices.
- I will keep learning new things.
- I will work hard toward my goals.
- I will treat others with kindness and respect.
- I will use my creativity to make a positive difference.
- I will keep going, even when challenges appear.
- I will never stop growing into the best version of myself.

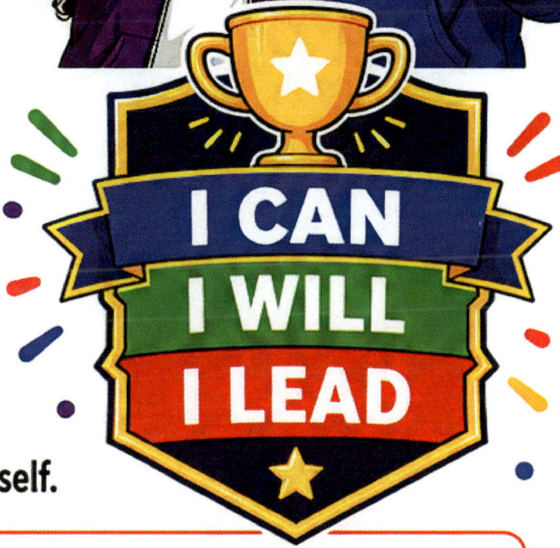

My Future Leader Signature

Name: ______________________

Date: ______________________

Signature: ______________________

My Biggest Goal Right Now

____

____

____

One Step I Will Take This Week

____

____

Why This Goal Matters to Me

____

____

FUTURE LEADERS MOTTO

DREAM BIG. LEARN MORE. LEAD BOLDLY. MAKE A DIFFERENCE.

The future belongs to those who prepare for it today.

The best investment you can make is in yourself.

ABOUT THE AUTHOR

Mona Liza Santos is an award-winning Filipina-American children's author, publisher, and founder of World Love Press. She is the author of more than 40 children's books focused on emotional literacy, kindness, confidence, resilience, and cultural identity.

Her work has been recognized by the **Mom's Choice Awards** for its positive impact on children and families.

Inspired by **motherhood, global travel**, and her **Filipino heritage**, Mona creates stories that encourage children to embrace who they are and recognize their worth.

She began her writing journey during the **pandemic** while creating comforting stories for her son during a time of uncertainty.

Having traveled to **more than 70 countries**, she brings a global and multicultural perspective to her storytelling while advocating for emotional wellness, empathy, and compassionate leadership in future

Stories have the power to heal, inspire, and change lives.

My heart is to help every child know they are valued, capable, and worthy of greatness.

BUDGET

www.monalizasantos.com

My Dream Big

Think big! What are your biggest dreams for the future?

What is my biggest dream?

Where do I see myself in the future?

What do I want to accomplish?

What kind of impact do I want to make?

Steps I Can Take to Make My Dreams Come True

1.
2.
3.
4.
5.

Who can support me on my journey?

What skills do I want to learn?

A note to my future self...

My Dream Big Notes

Future Savings Tracker

Think big! What are you saving for in the future?

My Savings Goal: ____________________ Goal Amount: $ ____________________

What am I saving for?

____
____
____
____

Why is this goal important to me?

____
____
____
____

How will I reach my goal?

- Start Date: ____________________
- Target Date: ____________________
- How much will I save each week/month?
  ____
- Ways I can save money:
  ____
  ____

Ideas to Help Me Save:

- ______________________________
- ______________________________
- ______________________________
- ______________________________
- ______________________________
- ______________________________

My Savings Progress

Date	Amount I Saved	Total Saved So Far	What I Did to Save

What will I do when I reach my goal?

____
____
____

How will achieving this goal make me feel?

____
____
____

Notes ______________________________
____
____
____
____

One Year Goal Tracker

Think about the next year! What do you want to achieve? Let's break it down.

My Big Goal for the Next 12 Months: ______________________

____

____

Why is this goal important to me?

____

____

____

____

How will achieving this goal help me?

____

____

____

____

Steps I will take to reach my goal:

- [ ] Step 1: ______________________
- [ ] Step 2: ______________________
- [ ] Step 3: ______________________
- [ ] Step 4: ______________________
- [ ] Step 5: ______________________

Resources or people that can help me:

____

____

____

Challenges I might face:

____

____

____

How I will celebrate when I reach my goal:

____

____

____

My Future Business Ideas

Think big! What kind of business would you love to create one day?

My Business Idea: ____________________

What problem will my business solve?

____
____
____
____

Who will my business help?

____
____
____
____

What products or services will I offer?

____
____
____
____

Why is this idea exciting to me?

____
____
____

Notes ____________________
____
____
____
____
____
____

NOTES

NOTES

You got this! Keep believing in yourself!

Teacher & Parent Answer Key

ANSWER KEY

Use this answer key to check understanding and encourage confident, smart choices!

Page 20

Saving: $20
Spending: $15
Giving: $5
Growing: $10

Percentages:

- Saving = 40%
- Spending = 30%
- Giving = 10%
- Growing = 20%

Total: 100%

Page 21

1. $15 (25% of $60)
2. $45
3. $6
4. $39

Bonus: $120

Page 34

1. Unnecessary Expense
2. Unnecessary Expense
3. Smart Purchase
4. Unnecessary Expense
5. Unnecessary Expense

Key Idea: A sale is only smart if you needed the item first.

Page 35

1. $40
2. $10
3. $30
4. $2.40
5. $32.40

Page 45

Income Skills:

- Drawing
- Tutoring
- Babysitting
- Cleaning
- Writing
- Crafting

Improve Skills: Practice regularly.

Sample Idea: Tutor younger students.

Page 47

1. $30 revenue
2. $12 costs
3. $18 profit
4. $48 profit
5. $9 savings

BIG PLANS!

Page 60

Revenue = $75
Profit = $50
Remaining = $30

Liam = $32
Ava = $25
Noah = $70

Page 70

1. Deposit
2. Balance
3. Debit Card
4. Withdrawal
5. Interest
6. Bank

Page 72

1. $450
2. $230
3. $470
4. Online purchase
5. Track spending

Page 73

1. $105
2. $120
3. Reach goals

Bonus: $120

Page 83

Gaming System →
✗ Avoid Purchase
Laptop →
✓ Borrow Responsibly
Designer Clothing →
✗ Avoid Purchase

Page 84

1. Smart choices
2. Build debt

Sample Rules:

- Borrow only when necessary.
- Pay on time.
- Keep debt low.

Page 85

1. $220
2. 4 months
3. $20

Bonus: 10 months

Page 86

1. Feels easy
2. Interest adds up
3. Planning avoids debt

Page 87

1. Borrow, save, or earn
2. Save first
3. Plan expenses
4. Buy it yourself

Page 96

Rent = $900
Groceries = $300
Utilities = $150
Transportation = $150
Savings = $500
Emergency Fund = $250
Entertainment = $250

Keep learning. Keep growing. Keep going!

Anything is possible for your future when you think money smart.

ANSWER KEY

Teacher & Parent Answer Key

Use this answer key to check understanding and encourage confident, smart choices!

Page 97

1. Needs
2. Yes
3. Save more
4. Stay on track

Page 98

Goal = New Bike

Cost = $300

Weekly Savings = $25

Time = 12 weeks

Page 99

1. Expenses add up
2. Control money
3. Save and plan ahead
4. Emergency fund

Page 102

1. Investing helps money grow
2. Growth takes time
3. Consistent saving helps growth

Page 103

1. Saving protects money
2. Stocks or business
3. Helps money grow

Sort It Out:

S, S, I, S, S, I, S, S, I

Page 104

1. Investing helps money grow
2. Growth takes time
3. Small growth adds up
4. Save and invest wisely

Page 106

1. Think long term
2. Builds wealth
3. Helps money grow
4. Save regularly

Page 108

6 Months = $120

12 Months = $240

24 Months = $480

Page 109

1. Saving consistently
2. Helps money grow
3. Spend less on wants

Page 110

1 Year = $180

3 Years = $540

Difference = $360

Problems:

1. $360
2. $900
3. $1,080
4. $600

Bonus = $640

Page 111

1. They want rewards now
2. Reach bigger goals
3. Saving and self-control

Activity:

1. $30 later
2. Study now
3. Save for bike
4. Focus on goals

Page 121

1. $300 revenue
2. $100 costs
3. $200 profit
4. $150 remaining

Entrepreneur Questions:

1. $400 profit
2. $175 profit
3. Advertising and new products

Plan today. Save wisely. Grow your future. You've got this!